AIR WAR GRENADA

An MC-130E Combat Talon aircraft during a low-level training mission. At least one of the 1st SOW MC-130s chosen to take part in URGENT FURY was equipped with the Fulton recovery system of the type fitted to the nose of the aircraft shown here. The system allows the in-flight pick-up of personnel from the ground by snagging a balloon-mounted line in the twin nose forks, here in the stowed position, after which the individual is winched aboard the recovery aircraft. The MC-130E is a special operations-dedicated aircraft, and is equipped with terrain-following radar, forward-looking infrared radar and an AN/ALQ-8 ECM pod.   USAF

AIR WAR GRENADA

By Stephen Harding

PICTORIAL HISTORIES PUBLISHING COMPANY, MISSOULA, MONTANA

LIBRARY OF CONGRESS
CATALOG CARD NUMBER 84-61935

ISBN 0-933126-52-2

First Printing   November 1984
Second Printing   March 1986

Cover Design: Allen Woodard
Typography: Arrow Graphics & Typography
Layout: Stan Cohen

FRONT COVER: An AC-130A Spectre gunship fires one of its 40mm cannon at a ground target. The -H model Spectres employed over Grenada were essentially similar in external appearance, though they had uprated engines, improved avionics and electronics, and were armed with a 105mm gun in place of one of the A model's two 40mm weapons.   USAF

BACK COVER: A few Army helicopters remained on Grenada for several months following the cessation of hostilities to support on-going American political and military assitance programs. These aircraft were, for the most part, the last remnants of the aviation forces used in Operation URGENT FURY.   DoD

PICTORIAL HISTORIES PUBLISHING COMPANY
713 South Third Street West
Missoula, Montana 59801

TABLE OF CONTENTS

ACKNOWLEDGMENTS

The author wishes to thank the following individuals and organizations, without whose help this work would have been far less complete: Jonathan Arms of the 1361st Audiovisual Squadron, USAF; the Books and Magazines Branch of the Air Force Office of Public Affairs; Ed Michalski of the Office of the Assistant Secretary of Defense for Public Affairs; William Rosenmund of the Office of the Chief of Public Affairs, U.S. Army; the staff of the Office of the Chief of Information, U.S. Navy; the Defense Audiovisual Agency; Don Hansen of McDonnell-Douglas; Bob Ferguson and Joe Dabney of Lockheed; Marylyn Phipps of Boeing; the public relations offices of Hughes Helicopters, Bell Helicopter-Textron and Sikorsky Aircraft; and Frank Colucci of *Defense Helicopter World*.

ABOUT THE AUTHOR

Stephen Harding is a military historian whose articles have appeared in popular and professional journals in both the United States and Great Britain. He is the author of *Gray Ghost: the RMS Queen Mary at War* and *Dominator: The Story of the B-32 Bomber*, and lives in Washington, D.C., with his wife, Mary, and daughter, Sarah.

PREFACE

Operation URGENT FURY, the October 1983 U.S. and Caribbean forces invasion of the island of Grenada, was a campaign whose origins, conduct and ultimate outcome were greatly influenced by the capabilities of modern military aircraft. This fact becomes self-evident when one considers the following points. First, the construction on Grenada of a runway capable of accommodating the latest Soviet-built reconnaissance and strike aircraft, aircraft capable of dominating the air and sea lanes of the entire Caribbean basin, was of very real concern to the United States government long before the political events on the island jeopardized the safety of the resident American citizens. Second, the vast majority of American and Caribbean Peacekeeping Force troops, equipment and supplies landed on Grenada during the course of URGENT FURY arrived by air. And, third, the ultimate success of the operation was, from the beginning, entirely dependent on the ability of U.S. military aircraft to transport, supply and protect those forces landed on Grenada in spite of initially intense anti-aircraft fire, inadequate facilities and the strain of almost continual operations.

This volume is not meant to be an exhaustive military history of Operation URGENT FURY, nor is it intended as an examination of U.S. foreign policy as practiced in the Caribbean basin. As its title indicates, this book is a pictorial record of the activities of Air Force, Navy, Marine and Army aviators and aircraft engaged in the initial assault on Grenada. The bulk of the information cited in this work was drawn from published accounts of the operation. However, much information regarding the planning and conduct of URGENT FURY remains classified for security reasons, and certain aspects of this account are therefore unavoidably vague. In those cases the author has relied upon informed supposition to flesh out this account of the most successful combat use of American airpower since the end of the Vietnam War.

Stephen Harding

PHOTO CREDITS

Photos credited USAF, USMC, USN, USA and DoD are official photos provided through the courtesy of, respectively, the U.S. Air Force, U.S. Marine Corps, U.S. Navy, U.S. Army and the U.S. Department of Defense. All other photos were supplied through the courtesy of the firm or individual credited.

BACKGROUND TO INVASION

PRIOR TO 1979 THE CARIBBEAN ISLAND OF GRENADA WAS RULED BY THE government of Sir Eric Gairy, a rather eccentric individual who had come to power immediately following the island's independence from Britain in February 1974. However, Gairy's erratic and bizarre behavior, coupled with his use of armed gangs to intimidate critics, soon led to the creation of several opposition political parties. In 1979 the largest of these groups, the socialist New Jewel Movement (NJM), took advantage of Gairy's temporary absence from Grenada to stage a near bloodless coup d'etat. Gairy was replaced as Prime Minister by Maurice Bishop, one of the leaders of NJM, who quickly began to reorganize the island's society along "revolutionary" socialist lines. Bishop suspended Grenada's 1974 constitution in favor of increasingly restrictive "People's Laws," exiled or imprisoned large numbers of political dissidents, and initiated close political, economic and military ties with the Soviet Union and Cuba.

Grenada's drift into the Soviet sphere of influence was of great concern to the United States and her allies, for the island's strategic location in the Caribbean basin made Grenada an ideal location for a Soviet/Cuban military base. Soviet bloc submarines and surface vessels operating from Grenada could easily disrupt the flow of American, Allied and neutral shipping from the Caribbean to the Atlantic, while reconnaissance and strike aircraft flying from airfields on the island could pose a serious threat to both military and commercial ships and aircraft throughout northern South America, most of Central America, and large parts of the Caribbean and central Atlantic Ocean. The increasingly evident buildup of Soviet Bloc and Cuban military personnel and equipment on Grenada during the period of 1980-82 seemed to validate the United States' concern, as did the construction of a major new airport complex at Point Salines on the island's southwest coast. The new airfield was of special concern, for though partially financed by a consortium that included both Canada and Mexico, the project's primary backer was the Cuban government. And though ostensibly intended solely for commercial use, the complex's design included such oddly non-commercial features as armored fuel storage tanks, military-style "hot-refuel" fuel transfer points embedded in the ramps, and several heavily reinforced concrete structures that looked ominously like ammunition storage bunkers. Finally, and most disturbing, it was obvious that the airfield's 9500-foot runway would be quite capable of accomodating the latest Soviet-built strike,

reconnaissance and transport aircraft.

Ironically, it was not Grenada's increasing militarization by the Soviet Union and Cuba that sparked the United States' eventual military intervention on the island. The cause was, instead, the disintegration of that very Grenadian government that had elicited such concern in Washington. On 12 October 1983 a long-simmering doctrinal dispute between Maurice Bishop and several members of his government flared into open conflict, and on the following day Bishop was placed under house arrest on the orders of his Deputy Prime Minister and major idealogical rival, Bernard Coard. Coard had secured the support of General Hudson Austin, the commander of Grenada's army, and thus felt he had the muscle necessary for a complete takeover. Coard was therefore rather surprised by the extent of public opposition to his bid for power, which was vividly demonstrated on 19 October when a large crowd of people freed the imprisoned Bishop. Coard and Austin struck back almost immediately, however, using troops and armored vehicles to break up a pro-Bishop rally held that same afternoon in the capital, St Georges. In the ensuing melee several unarmed civilians were killed and Bishop himself was recaptured. The former Prime Minister was then shot to death by a Lieutenant Abdullah.

The political upheaval that convulsed Grenada in the wake of the Coard-Austin coup elicited extreme concern in Washington, for it jeopardized the safety of more than 600 American medical students, tourists and retirees resident on the island. The possibility that some, or all, of these Americans might be siezed and held hostage by the Grenadian government, though considered remote, also had to be borne in mind. The United States government had no desire to find itself embroiled in a Caribbean replay of the 1979 Iranian hostage crisis, and planning was therefore begun for the evacuation of all Americans from Grenada. On 19 October the Joint Chiefs of Staff (JCS) issued a warning order to the Commander-in-Chief, Atlantic (CINCLANT), Admiral Wesley McDonald, for the execution on Grenada of a Non-combatant Evacuation Operation (NEO). At this point American planning envisioned a non-violent extraction conducted with the prior consent of the Grenadian government. This soon changed, however, for on 21 October the Organization of Eastern Caribbean States (OECS) formally asked Barbados, Jamaica and the United States to join with it in a military action

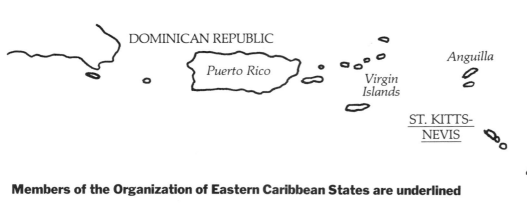

Members of the Organization of Eastern Caribbean States are underlined

CARIBBEAN AREA

intended to restore order and political stability to Grenada. The proposed action was to be conducted under the terms of a 1981 OECS treaty, which Organization member Grenada had signed, in which each member nation pledged to take whatever steps might be necessary to preserve the stability and security of the region. President Reagan and his advisors carefully weighed the OECS request for assistance in light of the United States' own continuing concern about the situation in Grenada, and the expanded operation received final Presidential approval on the evening of 21 October.

The decision to enlarge the Grenada action from a NEO to a full-scale combat assault was communicated to CINCLANT on the evening of 22 October. The purpose of the operation, as outlined in the JCS message, was threefold: first, to secure and evacuate resident American citizens, and certain other foreign nationals, in order to ensure their safety; second, to neutralize the Grenadian military and any other armed force present on the island that might threaten the evacuation process; and third, to restore order, stability and democracy to Grenada under the terms of the 1981 OECS treaty. The JCS message directed Admiral McDonald to undertake offensive operations on the island no later than 25 October, a requirement that allowed CINCLANT barely 48 hours in which to orchestrate the largest American combat action conducted since the end of the Vietnam War.

ESTIMATING ENEMY STRENGTH

UNITED STATES INTELLIGENCE SOURCES ESTIMATED THAT, AS OF 20 OCTOber, the Grenadian armed forces totaled approximately 3200 persons. Of this number, 600 were regular troops of the People's Revolutionary Army (PRA), while the remainder were members of the People's Revolutionary Militia (PRM), the police, the prison service, and so on. Plus, 700 members of a Cuban "construction battalion" were present in and around the Point Salines complex. This "construction battalion" was organized on military lines, was equipped with various types of small arms, and was known to include a large percentage of former Cuban Army regulars. It was not known how this sizable force would react to the American assault, but simple common sense dictated that the CINCLANT planners include it in their estimations of enemy strength. A further 50 Cubans were known to be serving as military advisors to the PRA and PRM, and it seemed safe to conclude that these highly motivated and professional soldiers would feel compelled to resist the landing of U.S. and Caribbean Peacekeeping Force (CPF) troops on Grenada.

Large Soviet and Cuban arms shipments to Grenada between 1979 and mid-October 1983 ensured that the island's defenders had a wide range of infantry weapons upon which to draw. These included such standard Soviet Bloc types as SKS rifles, AK-47 assault rifles, PPSh submachine guns, 7.62mm PKM light machine guns, 12.7mm DSHQ heavy machine guns, 82mm mortars and RPG-2/RGP-7 rocket-propelled grenades. Grenada was also known to have taken delivery of at least four BTR-60PB armored personnel carriers, each of which mounted a revolving tur-

ret housing a 14.5mm heavy and 7.62mm light machine gun. The island's anti-aircraft defenses were built around 25 ZU-23 wheeled, twin-barrel 23mm cannon, a few of which were thought to be radar-directed. These weapons had proved devastatingly effective against low-flying aircraft in a score of earlier conflicts, and were of special concern to the CINCLANT planning staff. Fortunately, however, Grenada had apparently not been equipped with the even more lethal SA-3 and SA-7 anti-aircraft missile systems normally supplied to Soviet client states.

The enemy troops and equipment actually present on Grenada were not the only worry facing URGENT FURY planners, for it was possible, though unlikely, that Cuba might attempt to intervene in the conflict. This was a not inconsequential threat, for by mid-October 1983 Cuba's military forces had become the strongest in Central America and the Caribbean basin. The Cuban Air Force consisted of nearly 400 aircraft, including such aging yet still potent types as MiG-17 and MiG-19 fighter-bombers and MiG-21 interceptors, as well as a squadron of Mi-24 helicopter gunships. The Cuban Navy was equally well-equipped with Soviet materiel, including three "Foxtrot"-class attack submarines, 25 "Osa" and "Komar"-class frigates and a mix of other patrol and support craft. And, finally, the Cuban Army could field over 100,000 well-trained and well-equipped regular troops, including two airborne battalions which specialized in commando-style operations. These quite considerable forces must have been of very real concern to URGENT FURY planners.

On 23 October several highly sophisticated E-3A Sentry AWACS AEW aircraft began monitoring all air activity over the Caribbean basin in preparation for the commencement of URGENT FURY. The aircraft, from TAC's 552d AWCW, utilized their pylon-mounted AN/APY-1 surveillance radar to detect and track both high- and low-level targets at ranges in excess of 230 miles.   USAF

BLUEPRINT FOR INVASION

THE FINAL OPERATIONAL PLAN FOR URGENT FURY, AS DEVELOPED BY the CINCLANT staff, outlined an essentially straightforward joint-services action adapted to the prevailing political and miltary conditions. According to the CINCLANT plan, the first American personnel ashore on Grenada would be reconnaissance teams of Navy SEALs and Army special operations forces. These teams would scout the proposed main-force landing zones, observe enemy activity and emplacements, and conduct offensive operations aimed at undermining the enemy's will and ability to resist. The main assault would consist of simultaneous Army and Marine landings on the east and west coasts of the island. The lead Marine element was to conduct a helicopter assault near Pearls Airport on the island's northeast coast, which would be followed by the landing of the main Marine force by amphibious vehicle. The Marines would be responsible for securing the north end of Grenada as well as the outlying island of Carriacou. The Army assault force, on the other hand, was to conduct either an airborne or air-land attack on the Point Salines airport complex, secure the airfield, and defend the area as a follow-on force of CPF and Army troops was landed by Air Force transports. The follow-on force would then move out from the airhead and secure the southern half of the island, evacuate those Americans and third-country nationals who wished to leave, and aid the CPF and Grenadians in reestablishing democracy on the island. Any close air support required during the

The USS *Guam*, shown here with the helicopters of HMM-261 embarked, was commissioned in 1965 and displaces 17,000 gross tons. The vessel was en route for NATO exercises off the coast of Spain and, ultimately, for duty off Lebanon, when ordered to steer for Grenada on 20 October.   USN

Top Right: The CH-53D Sea Stallion was by far the largest helicopter used by U.S. forces during the assault on Grenada; four of the heavy transport aircraft were embarked aboard *Guam* with HMM-261. In this view one of the Sea Stallions is seen running up its engines prior to the start of URGENT FURY. The large round pods carried on the small wing-like sponsons are auxiliary fuel tanks. Note also that the aircraft is equipped with two .50 M-2 machine guns, one mounted in the starboard access door and the other in the forward port-side window. DoD

Top Left: The predominant aircraft type in HMM-261's inventory during URGENT FURY was the CH-46E Sea Knight, 12 of which were operated in the medium transport role. This view of aircraft 157654 clearly shows the sponson-mounted ALE-39 chaff/flare dispenser fitted to all HMM-261 helicopters prior to the unit's departure for Lebanon. The device is intended to confuse the radar and infrared guidance systems of incoming anti-aircraft missiles by projecting brightly burning flares and clouds of radar-reflective chaff out to either side of the aircraft and thus decoy the missiles away from the aircraft. Also note that add-on armor plating has been fixed over some of the Sea Knight's more vulnerable areas, and that the aircraft is equipped with a .50 M-2 machine gun in the window just aft of the forward access door. The rounded object attached to the fuselage just above the machine gun is a stowed rescue hoist. DoD

Bottom: HMM-261 deployed four AH-1T Sea Cobra attack helicopters, identical to the one shown here, during URGENT FURY. The AH-1T is a twin-engined derivative of the Army AH-1G Cobra, and is intended for both infantry-support and anti-armor missions. The small nose-mounted turret directly above the three-barrelled M-197 20mm cannon houses a stabilized sight for use with the aircraft's weapon systems. The larger white cylinders seen here attached to the inboard hardpoints on the Sea Cobra's stub wings house 19 2.75-inch high explosive unguided rockets; the smaller cylinders mounted on the outboard pylons each contain seven white phosphorous rockets used as marking rounds. Bell Helicopter-Textron

course of the operation was to be supplied by Navy and Air Force fixed-wing aircraft and Marine helicopter gunships, and Air Force AWACS and fighter aircraft were to establish and enforce an aerial blockade intended to deter Cuban or Soviet intervention. The entire operation was programmed to take approximately 24 hours, depending of course on the amount of resistance encountered.

The military units used to flesh out the bare bones of the CINCLANT operational plan were drawn from a wide variety of sources. The naval force consisted of Marine Amphibious Unit 22 (22 MAU), which was itself made up of Battalion Landing Team 2/8 (BLT 2/8), headquarters and service elements, and Marine Medium Helicopter Squadron 261 (HMM 261). This last unit was a composite organization intended to fulfill 22 MAU's varying aviation requirements, and was equipped with 12 CH-46E Sea Knight medium transports, 4 CH-53D Sea Stallion heavy transports, 4 AH-1T Sea Cobra attack helicopters and 2 UH-1N light utility aircraft. The men and equipment of 22 MAU were embarked aboard the ships of Navy Amphibious Squadron 4 (PHIBRON 4), HMM 261 aboard the helicopter carrier *Guam*, and the ground elements dispersed among the landing ships *Barnstable County, Manitowoc* and *Trenton*. PHIBRON 4 had departed Norfolk, Virginia, on 18 October bound for NATO exercises off Spain and then for the waters off Lebanon. On 20 October the force was ordered to steer closer to Grenada, as was the carrier battle group accompanying it. This latter force was built around the aircraft carrier *Independence*, and included the cruiser *Richmond K. Turner* the guided missile destroyer *Coontz*, the destroyers *Caron* and *Moosbrugger*, and the guided missile frigate *Clifton Sprague*. The carrier battle group's aviation element, Carrier Air Wing 6 (CVW-6) aboard *Independence*, consisted of two attack squadrons (VA-15 and VA-87)

The aircraft carrier USS *Independence*, seen here during an exercise prior to the start of URGENT FURY, was destined to play a vital role in the assault on Grenada. Her embarked air wing would provide ASW and EW support for the U.S. task force, as well as on-call close air support and SAR. Like *Guam* and her supporting ships, *Independence* and her accompanying battle group were en route for Spain and Lebanon when diverted toward Grenada on 20 October.

USN

THE INVASION OF GRENADA

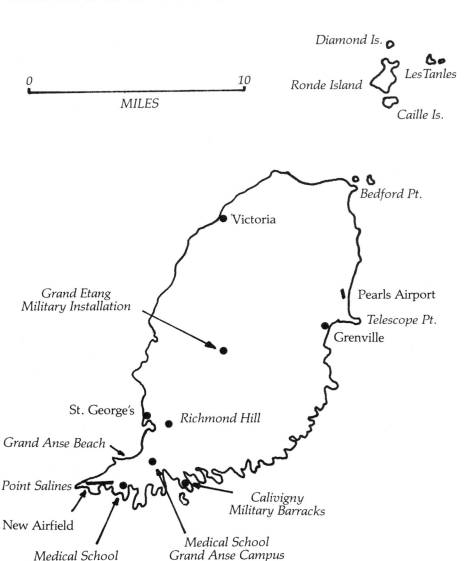

Diamond Is.

Ronde Island   Les Tanles

Caille Is.

0 ——————————— 10
MILES

Bedford Pt.

Victoria

Grand Etang
Military Installation

Pearls Airport

Telescope Pt.
Grenville

St. George's   Richmond Hill

Grand Anse Beach

Point Salines

Calivigny
Military Barracks

New Airfield

Medical School
Grand Anse Campus

Medical School
True Blue Campus

equipped with A-7E Corsair II aircraft, one attack squadron (VA-176) flying A-6E Intruders, two fighter squadrons (VF-14 and VF-32) with F-14A Tomcats, an anti-submarine patrol squadron (VS-28) of S-3A Vikings, an E-2C Hawkeye-equipped airborne early warning (AEW) squadron (VAW-122), a tactical electronic warfare squadron (EW) (VAQ-131) flying EA-6B Prowlers, and a helicopter anti-submarine warfare (ASW) squadron (HS-15) with SH-3H Sea Kings.

The Air Force units chosen to participate in URGENT FURY were drawn from several USAF major commands, including Tactical Air Command (TAC), Strategic Air Command (SAC) and the Military Airlift Command (MAC). The need to transport large numbers of men and thousands of tons of equipment to Grenada and other nearby Caribbean islands meant that MAC was the most heavily tasked of these three major commands. Indeed, MAC's eventual role in the operation was so large that aircraft had to be drawn from 15 separate regular and reserve units belonging to four different numbered Air Forces. Six of these units were equipped with variants of the C-130 Hercules: three tactical airlift wings (TAWs) flying the E model transport, one TAW flying the H model, one reserve tactical airlift group (TAG), also with the E model, and one special operations squadron (SOW) flying AC-130H Spectre gunships and MC-130E Combat Talon assault transport aircraft. Another seven of the MAC units assigned to URGENT FURY were military airlift wings (MAWs), five regular and two reserve, flying the C-141B Starlifter jet transport. The last two MAC units, one regular and one reserve, were MAWs equipped with the huge C-5A Galaxy. Tactical Air Command, for its part, was tasked to provide one tactical fighter wing (TFW) of F-15 Eagles, one airborne warning and control wing (AWCW) flying E-3A Sentries, and an electronic warfare group of the Pennsylvania Air National Guard with specially equipped EC-130E "Coronet Solo II" EW aircraft. Strategic Air Command's contribution to URGENT FURY was to consist of two KC-10A Extender air-refueling tankers in addition to the aerial reconnaissance platforms that had played such an important role in pre-strike planning.

The Army units earmarked for use in URGENT FURY were, like those of the Navy, Marines and Air Force, drawn from a wide variety of locations and parent organizations. The initial assault on the Point Salines area was to be conducted by elements of the 1st and 2d Battalions, 75th (Ranger) Infantry, acting in concert with other Army and joint-services special operations forces. The Rangers were to either airdrop or airland, whichever seemed best suited to the prevailing tactical situation, and secure the runway prior to the arrival of the follow-on force. This force, consisting of elements of the 82d Airborne Division, would then airland at Point Salines and move out from there to secure the rest of southern Grenada. Four Army aviation units were tasked to support these initial actions. The largest of the units was the 82d Airborne Division's 82d Combat Aviation Battalion (82d CAB), equipped with a mix of UH-60 Blackhawk transport helicopters, UH-1H Iroquois command and control (C&C) and utility aircraft, and AH-1S Cobra gunships. Another Fort Bragg-based unit, the 1st Squadron, 17th Cavalry (1/17 CAV), was to provide OH-58C Kiowa observation helicopters in addition to its own Blackhawks and Cobras. Army aeromedical evacuation duty on the island was to be the responsibility of the 57th Medical Detachment, an air ambulance unit equipped with specially modified UH-60s. The special operations forces deployed to Grenada were, according to a post-campaign ariticle in the authoritative journal *Defense Helicopter World*, to be supported by elements of the 160th Aviation Battalion from Fort Campbell, Kentucky. This unit, an experimental light air cavalry organization, was apparently tasked to support the special operations forces with several Hughes Helicopter model 500MD Defenders. These aircraft are updated, heavily armed scout and observation models of the Vietnam-era OH-6 Cayuse, and the 160th Aviation Battalion (160th AB) is thought to be the only Army unit so equipped. In addition to these units various other Army aviation organizations were tasked to supply individual pilots, crewmen and aircraft on an "as-needed" basis.

Two of Carrier Air Wing Six's three attack squadrons were equipped with A-7E Corsair II aircraft identical to the one shown here. The single-seat, single-engine Corsair II is armed with an internal 20mm cannon and is capable of carrying up to 15,000 pounds of ordnance on six wing hardpoints. USN

The third attack squadron embarked aboard *Independence* was equipped with the A-6E Intruder. The VA-52 aircraft illustrated here displays the Intruder's characteristic side-by-side cockpit seating and fixed air-to-air refueling probe. The twin-engine A-6E can carry up to 18,000 pounds of ordnance on its various wing and fuselage hardpoints. The KA-6D air tanker version, four of which served aboard *Independence* during operations off Grenada, carries external fuel tanks and air refueling equipment in lieu of weapons. USN

Three of VF-32's F-14A Tomcats in flight prior to the start of the Grenada assault. This unit and VF-14 were tasked with the air defense of the U.S. task force. The threat of enemy air attack, though remote, was nonetheless considered very real.   USN

Top Left: *Independence's* air group included four EA-6B Prowler electronic warfare aircraft of VAQ-131. As the VAQ-129 aircraft shown here illustrates, the EA-6B is capable of carrying up to five AN/ALQ-99 electronic jamming pods on its four wing and one fuselage hardpoint. Additional ECM equipment is housed in the large pod atop the aircraft's tail. The Prowler has a crew of four, two men seated side-by-side in each of two cockpits.　　　　USN

Top Right: A VS-28 S-3A Viking recovers aboard *Independence*. This squadron was to provide ASW support for the U.S. task force, though its aircraft were also destined to serve as aerial enforcers of the government's initial news media ban.　　　　USN

Bottom: The four E-2C Hawkeyes of VAW-122 were tasked to provide round-the-clock AEW support for the task force throughout the course of URGENT FURY. This view of one of the squadron's aircraft gives a good impression of the size of the radome housing the Hawkeye's AN/APA-171 radar.　　　　USN

Top Left: An SH-3H Sea King ASW helicopter, six of which served aboard *Independence* with HS-15. The helicopter carries a wide range of submarine detection devices, including dipping sonor, air-dispensed sonobuoys, and MAD. The aircraft is normally armed with a mix of depth charges and anti-submarine torpedoes.   Sikorsky Aircraft

Top Right: An Army UH-60A Blackhawk utility helicopter in flight. This type equipped at least two, and possibly three, of the Army aviation units chosen to participate in the Grenada assault. All of the UH-60s deployed to Grenada, except those of the 57th Med Det, were equipped with two .50 cal M-2 or two 7.62mm M-60 machine guns. The weapons were mounted in the sliding windows on either side of the aircraft just aft of the cockpit.   Sikorsky Aircraft

Bottom: Several UH-1H Iroquois helicopters like the one shown here served on Grenada during the course of URGENT FURY. The aircraft operated in the light utility, C&C and observation roles, and most were equipped with at least one door-mounted machine gun.   Bell Helicopter-Textron

Top Left: The OH-58C Kiowa observation helicopter also served on Grenada, equpping A Troop, 1/17 CAV.　Bell Helicopter-Textron

Top Right: The AH-1S Cobra attack helicopter equipped two Army aviation units on Grenada. As shown here, the single-engine AH-1S is armed with the same M197 20mm cannon that equips Marine Corps AH-1T aircraft, and carries the same TOW missiles and nose-mounted sight. Note that the Cobra's engine exhaust port is fitted with an extended shroud in order to reduce the aircraft's infrared signature. The small cylindrical object mounted above the exhaust shroud is an AN/ALQ-144 infrared jammer of the same type fitted to HMM-261's helicopters.　Bell Helicopter-Textron

Bottom: The special operations forces chosen to participate in URGENT FURY are thought to have been supported by a mixed force of OH-6 Cayuse and 500MD Defender helicopters operated by the 160th Aviation Battalion from Fort Campbell, Kentucky. The two aircraft are externally very similar. The aircraft shown here is a 500MD Defender fitted with a mast-mounted optical sight, a feature not found on the Cayuse/Defender aircraft apparently used in Grenada. The Defender differs from the Cayuse in several ways, one of the more obvious of which is rearrangement of the engine exhaust. The Cayuse's exhaust is located at the rear of the main aircraft body, immediately below the tail boom root. The Defender, on the other hand, utilizes the "Black Hole" infrared signature suppression system fitted to the aircraft shown here. The system redirects the engine exhaust through two small ducts, one on either side of the main aircraft body about three feet aft of the rear door. The Cayuse and Defender aircraft thought to have been used on Grenada also differed from the aircraft shown here in that they were equipped with machine gun and rocket pods fitted just below the rear doors on both sides of the aircraft.

Hughes Helicopters

At least half of the MAC units tasked to provide airlift support for URGENT FURY were equipped with the C-141B Starlifter, a lengthened version of the original C-141A. The aircraft shown here sports the newly adopted "European 1" camouflage scheme, though several of the Starlifters which participated in the assault on Grenada were uncamouflaged.

Lockheed Aircraft

THE WORD IS "GO"

ON THE MORNING OF SUNDAY, 23 OCTOBER, THE AMERICAN PEOPLE awoke to the news that the Marine Battalion Landing Team on duty with the Multinational Peacekeeping Force in Beirut had been the target of a tragically successful terrorist bomb attack. The news of the bombing prompted President Reagan to cut short an official visit to Georgia and return immediately to Washington, where he called an emergency meeting of the National Security Planning Group. The ultimate fate of URGENT FURY was a major topic of discussion at this meeting, for the launch of a large-scale U.S. combat assault in the Caribbean so soon after the Lebanon tragedy might well have been perceived as a case of misdirected anger. Such a perception, however inaccurate, could have damaged American prestige and interests worldwide. President Reagan nonetheless decided that the need to protect American citizens on Grenada, and to assist the OECS in restoring order and political stabilty to the island, had to take precedence. On the afternoon of 23 October Mr. Reagan therefore directed that URGENT FURY proceed as planned.

URGENT FURY DAY BY DAY:

23 OCTOBER (D-2)

The President's "GO" order sparked a flurry of activity at military bases across the United States. At McChord AFB, Washington, elements of the 2d Battalion, 75th Infantry (Ranger) from nearby Fort Lewis boarded Air Force C-141B Starlifter transports for the flight to Hunter Army Air Field (AAF), Georgia. There the men of the 2d Battalion would join up with their fellow Rangers of the 1st Battalion prior to their joint departure for Grenada.

The C-141Bs transporting the men of the 2d Ranger Battalion to Georgia were not the only Air Force aircraft involved in URGENT FURY-related activities on 23 October. Earlier in the day several E-3A Sentry AWACs aircraft of the 552d AWCW at Tinker AFB, Oklahoma, had taken off on the first of many patrols over the Caribbean basin. These highly sophisticated airborne early warning (AEW) aircraft were to monitor all Cuban and Soviet air activity in the Caribbean and thus help enforce an aerial blockade of Grenada aimed at preventing Cuban reinforcements from reaching the island. If the AWACS aircraft detected any such attempt they were to vector F-15 Eagle interceptors toward the intruders. The F-15s tasked to undertake these interceptions were drawn from the 33d TFW at Eglin AFB, Florida, and they deployed to a forward operating base at Naval Air Station (NAS) Roosevelt Roads, Puerto Rico, at about the same time the first E-3A took up its patrol station. Barksdale AFB in Louisiana also launched aircraft in support of URGENT FURY on 23 October, for two KC-10A Extender air tankers of the base's resident 2d Bombardment Wing (2d BW) had been chosen to provide aerial refuelling support for aircraft engaged in URGENT FURY-related activities.

Many Navy organizations also spent 23 October preparing for the commencement of URGENT FURY. On board both *Guam* and *Independence*, maintenance teams worked to prepare helicopters and fixed-wing attack aircraft for possible battle in the coming operation, while the E2Cs of VAW-122 and S-3As of VS-28 undoubtedly maintained their normal vigilance around the carrier battle group. At Norfolk, the evening of 23 October saw the activation of Joint Task Force 120 (JTF 120), the organization that would be the overall command group for the Grenada operation. Vice Admiral Joseph Metcalf III was named commander of JTF 120 upon its activation, and he immediately dispatched several senior members of his planning staff to the *Guam*.

24 OCTOBER (D-1)

Most of the military organizations slated to participate in URGENT FURY spent 24 October making final preparations, and late in the evening men of the 1st and 2d Battalions, 75th Infantry, began boarding Air Force transports at Hunter Army Air Field for the five-hour flight to Grenada. The Rangers were divided into two waves spread among 12 aircraft. The first wave consisted of elements of the 1st Battalion, and was loaded aboard seven aircraft. The first two of these aircraft were specially-equipped MC-130E "Combat Talon" transports from the Air Force's 1st Special Operations Wing (1st SOW) at Hurlburt Field, Florida. The MC-130Es bore the men of Company A of the 1st Battalion, who were tasked with the initial seizure and clearance of the Point Salines runway. The third through seventh aircraft, all of which were standard C-130E transports, carried the remainder of the 1st Battalion. Aircraft number 3 was to drop its Rangers 30 minutes after the troops from the two MC-130Es had landed, while the remaining four aircraft would airdrop or airland their embarked Rangers, whichever the tactical situation would allow. The second wave of aircraft, five C-130Es, carried the men of the 2d Battalion and were to either airdrop or land the men as the situation dictated. The first wave of seven aircraft departed Hunter AAF shortly after 2130 hours local time, followed about 20 minutes later by the five aircraft of the second wave.

The 1st SOW had been tasked to provide AC-130H Spectre gunships to support URGENT FURY and several of these aircraft, belonging to the Wing's 16th Special Operations Squadron (16th SOS), departed Hurlburt Field at about the same time the troop transports were leaving Hunter AAF. The Spectres each carried 18- to 20-man crews instead of the normal 14 in order to provide a longer presence over the target zone, and each aircraft was scheduled to be refueled several times by the 2d BW KC-10A Extenders. This would further increase each gunship's "loiter time" over Grenada.

At the same time the Rangers were beginning their journey to Grenada, the first Navy SEAL teams were actually going ashore on the island's northeast coast. The Marine assault on the area near Pearls Airfield was scheduled to be conducted by landing craft and amphibious vehicle, and it was therefore vital that the operational commanders aboard *Guam* know the exact condition of the designated landing beaches. The SEALs were sent ashore to find out, and were inserted by Zodiac inflatable boats.

25 OCTOBER (D-DAY)

The opening day of Operation URGENT FURY began with bad news. The SEAL teams inserted onto the northeast coast late on the night of 24 October had conducted a complete beach reconnaissance and, at about 0300 hours, reported that the designated landing sites were completely unsuitable for landing craft and amphibious vehicles. The planning staff aboard *Guam* thus had to make some rapid recalculations, and soon settled on a modification of the original plan. The lead Marine elements would still go in by helicopter, but the follow-on units would switch from a beach landing to a helicopter assault. In order to conduct the attack before dawn the troops would have to be loaded aboard HMM 261's helos and on their way to the landing zone (LZ) before 0415.

While the Marines aboard *Guam* and the other landing vessels off the northeast coast were preparing to board their helicopters the first Air Force aircraft arrived over the southern end of the island. A single AC-130H made a high-speed pass over the Point Salines complex to examine the runway for obstacles and determine the extent of the anti-aircraft artillery (AAA) threat. The Spectre's crew used low-light televisions cameras and various infrared and electronic sensors to scan the area below, and determined that much of the runway was blocked by construction equipment and light vehicles. The AC-130H also attracted considerable AAA fire, though on-board sensors indicated that the enemy guns were apparently not radar-directed as some URGENT FURY planners had feared. The gunship radioed its findings to the inbound transports, and probably to EC-130E Airborne Battlefield Command and Control Center (ABCCC) aircraft orbiting offshore as well, and then turned back out to sea.

While the AC-130H was probing the Point Salines defenses the men of Company E, 2d Battalion, 8th Marines (2/8 Marines) were boarding HMM 261's CH-46E Sea Knight helicopters for the assault on Pearls airfield. All six helicopters of the first wave had started the run into the LZ when a sudden rain squall forced them back to the *Guam*. The helicopters were directed to remain aboard ship until the weather cleared, and the assault was postponed until 0500. The forced delay was communicated to the inbound Air Force transports, which then went into a circular orbit offshore so as not to arrive over Point Salines before the Marines had begun their landings in the north. A few minutes later the transports were informed that the weather off the northeast coast had still not cleared, and the take-off of the Marine helicopters was therefore slipped to 0500. This second postponement was greeted with some relief aboard the lead MC-130E, for it gave the aircraft's crew additional time to deal with a sudden malfunction in the on-board navigational system.

At exactly 0500 the CH-46s bearing the men of Company E lifted off from the *Guam* and, escorted by all four Sea Cobras, headed for Landing Zone (LZ) Buzzard, an open area 700 meters south of Pearls airport. This site had been chosen after intelligence reports indicated that the runway area was defended by several ZU-23s, though it quickly became apparent that LZ Buzzard was not without its own defenses. The lead Sea Knight began drawing AAA fire as it neared touch down, and the volume of fire increased as the rest of the helos followed the leader in. The door gunners

in each helicopter returned fire with their .50 caliber machine guns while the Sea Cobras bored in on the AAA sites with 20mm cannon fire. The PRA gun crews soon abandoned their weapons in the face of such determined fire, and the guns themselves were later captured by the advancing Marines.

At the same time the Marines were starting to fan out from LZ Buzzard, the first Rangers were leaving their aircraft over Point Salines. The Lead MC-130 started its run at 0536, and all of Company A was out the door within 90 seconds. However, the second aircraft was met by a hail of AAA fire, and the pilot understandably aborted his run. An orbiting Spectre gunship called in to suppress the enemy fire unleashed a hail of 20mm, 40mm and 105mm rounds on the various gun sites, while the troop transports orbited just offshore. The second MC-130 Talon resumed its

The first U.S. aircraft over Grenada on the morning of D-Day was an AC-130H Spectre gunship of the 1st SOW. As depicted here, repeated refuelings by the 2d BW KC-10A tankers enabled the AC-130s to spend extended periods of time in the air over and near Grenada. At least one of the engaged Spectres refueled three times in this manner, staying aloft for nearly 16 hours.   USAF

Top Left: Deck scene aboard *Guam* on the morning of D-Day. HMM-261's helicopters had originally lifted off for the assault on Pearls airport before 0430, but were forced back to the ship by bad weather. This photo shows deck crewmen and flight personnel waiting to resume flight operations. DoD

Top Right: By 0445 the weather had improved enough to allow the resumption of flight operations. Here two CH-46E Sea Knights run up their engines as their crew chiefs await the arrival on deck of the Marine assault troops. DoD

Bottom: Loading up. Men of Company G, 2/8 Marines board an HMM-261 Sea Knight via the aircraft's lowered tail ramp. DoD

Top Left: One of the HMM-261's four AH-1T Sea Cobras runs up its engines as deck crew men top off its fuel tanks prior to liftoff for the assault on Pearls airport. The aircraft carries two TOW tubes, a 2.75-inch rocket pod and an ALE-39 flare/chaff dispenser on each stub wing. This view also clearly shows the twin engine exhausts that distinguish this type from the Army AH-1S, as well as the AN/ALQ-144 infrared jammer common to both aircraft.   DoD

Top Right: Another AH-1T lifts off to escort the first assault wave. This aircraft has been equipped with a different type of single-cell TOW launcher on the outboard hardpoint. This photo also shows the chin-mounted M197 20mm cannon to good advantage, as well as the nose-mounted stabilized TOW sight. In both Army and Marine Corps Cobras the pilot occupies the rear seat while the gunner sits in the forward position.   DoD

Bottom: The first wave of Sea Knights en route to LZ Buzzard, an open area about 700 meters south of Pearls airport.   DoD

aborted run into the drop zone at 0550, closely followed by the five C-130s carrying the remaining elements of the 1st Battalion, all of which were on the ground by 0600.

Other American units began arriving on Grenada at the same time the 1st Ranger Battalion was attempting to consolidate its position at Point Salines. To the north, HMM 261's Sea Knights were inserting the men of Company F, 2/8 Marines into LZ Oriole near the coastal town of Grenville. This landing was essentially unopposed, and the Marines were able to move out quickly toward their objectives. American special operations forces were not so fortunate, however, when they attempted to assault Fort Rupert and the Governor General's Residence near the capital of St. Georges. The attack on Fort Rupert, which began at approximately 0610, ran into stiff opposition and quickly began to bog down, while the force assaulting the Governor General's Residence was met with equally withering fire. The attempt to neutralize the PRA forces holding the fort was abandoned, though the special operations team assigned to reach and protect Governor General Scoon had no choice but to press on with their attack against PRA/PM forces surrounding the Residence. Some air support was apparently provided at this point by the Cayuse/Defender aircraft organic to the special operations forces, though this cannot be verified.

By 0635 the 1st Ranger Battalion had managed to clear most of the obstacles from the runway at Point Salines, despite heavy incoming mortar and small arms fire. The need to suppress this fire before the 2d Ranger Battalion could land led the 1st Battalion commander to once again call upon the AC-130H gunships orbiting just outside effective AAA range. The Spectres moved back in toward the hills to the north and east of the airport complex, and orbiting just above the maximum effective range of the ZU-23 AAA, poured 20mm and 40mm cannon fire into the enemy positions. The immense volume of fire put out by the AC-130H weapons systems was used to devastating effect against identified AAA sites, mortar positions and trench lines, though the Ranger forces continued to receive incoming fire from various points around their perimeter.

Enemy fire was also heavy in the area around Richmond Hill Prison, and it was all directed at the American special operations teams that had begun assaulting the PRA strongpoint just after 0700. Indeed, the enemy resistance was so fierce that the attack on the prison complex had to be aborted. The team assigned to rescue Sir Paul Scoon was also running into increasingly stiff opposition. An attempt to land personnel on the roof of the Governor General's Residence by helicopter had to be abandoned when the aircraft came under intense automatic weapons fire that wounded three crew members. The special operations team was also fac-

Approaching the LZ. This photo shows the crew chief of a first wave Sea Knight manning the starboard machine gun and scanning the nearing LZ for any sign of trouble.   DoD

Port side machine gun on the same CH-46E. The weapon is a venerable M-2 .50 heavy machine gun. The basin below it is intended to catch spent cartridge cases and thus keep them from littering the inside of the aircraft.   DoD

Top Left: Having just off-loaded its cargo of Marines, this CH-46E has just lifted off for the return to *Guam*. One crewman mans the window-mounted heavy machine gun while a second stands by with his individual M-16 rifle.　　　DoD

Top Right: Marines of Company G advance off LZ Buzzard as the Sea Knight that delivered them passes overhead.　　　DoD

Bottom: The first Rangers began parachuting onto the runway at Point Salines within minutes of the Marine landings at LZ Buzzard. The Rangers departed the C-130s at an altitude of just 500 feet in order to minimize their exposure to the intense ground fire that greeted the first wave of aircraft.　　　USA

The major threat to U.S. aircraft engaged in operations over Grenada during URGENT FURY came from ZU-23 AA guns like the one show here overlooking Point Salines. Several C-130 aircraft were holed by rounds from these weapons during the initial assault, and strikes by AC-130H gunships and Navy attack aircraft were required to silence the enemy guns. Note that this particular weapon is surrounded by spent cartridge cases, indicating that it has seen action. The ZU-23 has a maximum effective range of about 8,000 feet, and each barrel can fire over 200 rounds of armour-piercing, incendiary or ball/tracer ammunition per minute. (DoD)

ed with the very real threat posed by the imminent arrival of several BTR-60PB APCs, and thus terminated their direct assault and began looking for other ways into the Governor's Residence.

At 0725, just about the time the special operations force helicopter aborted its landing on the roof of the Governor's Residence, the commander of Company E, 2/8 Marines, reported that Pearls airport was secure. This encouraging news was followed 15 minutes later by the arrival at Point Salines of the first C-130 bearing men of the 2d Ranger Battalion. The four Hercules transports carrying the rest of the Battalion were all on the ground within the next 20 minutes, and by 0845 both Ranger units were ready to move out from the airhead in force. Within the next half hour Company A, 1/75 had secured the True Blue medical school campus at the east end of the Point Salines complex, to the immense relief of several hundred medical students. The rest of the 1st Ranger Battalion then moved to secure the high ground along a ridge to the north of the airport complex, while the men of the 2d Battalion prepared to advance from the runway, cross through the 1st Battalion's lines, and move toward the Calivigny Barracks area to the east of True Blue.

While the two Ranger battalions were moving out of the Point Salines complex the Marines were busy securing their areas of responsibility to the north. Company F, 2/8 Marines had not encountered any resistance during the advance through Grenville, and the city was officially secured just before 0900. Soon thereafter the wisdom of inserting the Marine forces by helicopter rather than over-the-beach assault was confirmed in a most dramatic way. A single LVTP-7 amphibious armored personnel carrier was dispatched toward shore from one of the PHIBRON 4 vessels lying just off Grenville. The LVTP, crewed by a top driver and vehicle commander, barely managed to make it across the reefs and shifting sand that fronts Grenada's entire eastern coast. The demonstration made it all too obvious that a full amphibious assault, had it been necessary, might well have been a debacle if resisted by even a small force of PRA troops.

By 0930 the Ranger advance out of the greater Point Salines area was well under way. Resistance from PRA and Cuban forces was stiff, though apparently uncoordinated, and repeated strikes by AC-130s and Navy A-7E and A-6E attack aircraft helped clear the way for the advancing Rangers. The battle was not entirely in the Americans' favor however, a fact that was tragically proven when five Rangers riding in a jeep were ambushed by a PRA squad. Four of the Americans were killed outright, while the fifth was barely able to make it back to the Ranger lines to report the attack. The PRA troops responsible for the ambush were quickly located and engaged, and surrendered after only a brief firefight. A few minutes later another Ranger squad captured intact one of the

A-7E Corsair II aircraft launch from *Independence*. Strikes by Navy attack aircraft were instrumental in breaking up PRA and Cuban counter-attacks near Point Salines on D-Day.

USN

ZU-23 AA guns that had been firing on U.S. aircraft and, in a moment of inspired improvisation, turned the weapon against a Cuban strong point that was holding up the American advance. The high volume of fire from the ZU-23, combined with repeated strafing runs by the American aircraft, convinced the Cubans that further resistance was hopeless, and 275 surrendered to a small group of Rangers. The Cubans turned over an array of small arms, mortars, recoilless rifles and assorted ammunition, and were marched away to a detention area near the Point Salines runway. This mass capitulation did not mark the end of PRA and Cuban resistance, however, for several hundred well-armed enemy troops still remained at large on the southern end of Grenada.

The determination displayed by many PRA troops was well demonstated in the continuing battle for the Governor General's Residence near St. Georges. By 1000 the special operations forces assigned to assault the Residence had managed to overcome the PRA resistance and enter the mansion, only to then be besieged by a newly arrived force of PRA reinforcements. The enemy troops renewed their assault on the American forces, though the roles had now been reversed: the special operations teams were inside the Residence while the PRA was outside trying to get in. At about 1025 the PRA was reinforced by at least two and possibly as many as four BTR-60s, which began to methodically decimate the mansion's facade with their heavy machine guns. The besieged U.S. troops put out an urgent call for air support, which was answered by the arrival at 1045 of two of HMM 261's AH-1T Sea Cobras. The attack helicopters strafed the PRA troops surrounding the Governor's Residence, and used cannon and rocket fire to force the BTRs away from the mansion. One BTR was destroyed by the Sea Cobras and the others were forced to change position so often that the effectiveness of their fire was greatly reduced.

The Marine landings near Pearls airport encountered only scattered resistance and the entire assault force was soon on the ground. Here one of HMM-261's four CH-53D Sea Stallions disgorges a final group of Marines at LZ Buzzard. Note that the man just exiting the aircraft is armed with an M-72 LAW anti-tank rocket in addition to his M-16.   DoD

Top Left: A Cubana Airlines Antonov AN-26B Curl short-haul transport. This aircraft arrived on Grenada on 24 October bearing Cuban Army Colonel Pedro Tortolo, who had been dispatched from Havana to lead a spirited defense against the anticipated U.S. assault. Tortolo was something less than successful; indeed, he sought refuge in the Soviet embassy almost immediately after his arrival on the island. After his eventual repatriation to Cuba, Tortolo was tried for cowardice on the orders of Fidel Castro, found guilty, and sent to fight with the Cuban expeditionary force in Angola as a private soldier.　　　　　　　　　　　　　　　　　　　DoD

Top Right: Three PRA BTR-60PB armored personnel carriers attempted a counterattack near Point Salines on the afternoon of D-Day. The two shown here were destroyed by 90mm recoilless rifle fire, while the third was knocked out a short time later by either an AC-130 or a Navy A-7.　　　　DoD

Bottom: The Cuban construction workers at Point Salines attempted to turn their barracks area into a strongpoint, but abandoned the idea after repeated American air strikes. This photo shows the effects on the barracks buildings of both Spectre 105mm cannon fire and Ranger small arms fire.　　　DoD

Air Force C-130s and C-141s began landing additional troops at Point Salines even though the runway was still subject to hostile fire. Here an MAC C-130 starts its take-off roll only minutes after off-loading its cargo of troops.

DoD

HMM-261 also deployed two UH-1N light utility helicopters aboard *Guam*. The aircraft are twin-engined derivatives of the famous UH-1 "Huey" and are used for command and control duties, general liaison and observation. Unlike the aircraft illustrated here, the UH-1Ns used by HMM-261 during URGENT FURY sported low-visibility olive drab markings.

Bell Helicopter-Textron

Both the 436th and 512th MAWs operated C-5A Galaxy heavy transports in support of URGENT FURY. The huge aircraft were used primarily to transport Army helicopters from Pope AFB to Barbados. Several of the C-5As seen at Grantly Adams airport wore the "European 1" camouflage illustrated here.
USAF

A KC-10A Extender refuels an F-15C Eagle. Two Extenders from the 2d Bomb Wing at Barksdale AFB, Louisiana, were detached for service in support of URGENT FURY.   USAF

The Army unit intended to undertake the majority of MEDEVAC duties on Grenada, the 57th Medical Detachment, was equipped with UH-60A Blackhawks like the one shown here. The aircraft are specially-equipped for casualty-evacuation, and are prominently marked with red crosses to indicate their non-combatant status. Sikorsky Aircraft

A Marine poses next to one-half of all enemy aircraft found on Grenada. This particular machine is a Russian-built Antonov AN-2P Colt in the markings of Aeroflot Soviet Airlines.   DoD

Pearls airport was also used as a receiving point for men and equipment deployed to Grenada. Here a C-130 prepares to unload cargo in front of the small terminal building. A Marine CH-46E sits just in front of the MAC aircraft, and the Aeroflot AN-2P Colt and Cubana AN-26B Curl sit idle just behind the Sea Knight.

DoD

Psychological warfare operations continued on Grenada even after the shooting stopped, and were supported by both MC-130E Combat Talon and EC-130E Coronet Solo II aircraft. The latter type, flown by the 193d Electronic Combat Group of the Pennsylvania Air National Guard, is shown here. Note the large black antenna arrays just forward of the aircraft's tail and on the outboard wing section. The black and white pod outboard of the port wing antenna carries ECM equipment.

USAF

Among the last duties carried out on Grenada by Marine helicopters was the transfer of large captured weapons to central storage facilities. Here an HMM-261 Sea Stallion approaches a ZU-23 mount prior to sling-loading the weapon for transfer to Point Salines on 29 October.   DoD

The Sea Cobras soon got another chance to prove their value in the air support role. At about 1200 two of the aircraft were ordered to return to the *Guam*, rearm, refuel, and then head toward Fort Frederick to support the renewed special operations force attack on the strong point. The two attack helicopters, one crewed by Captains Timothy Howard and Jeb Seagle, the other by Captain John Giguere and First Lieutenant J.R. Sharver, arrived over the embattled fort at about 1245 and immediately began attacking the site with TOW missiles, cannon and rockets. The fire poured into the fort by the two Sea Cobras silenced some of the opposition, but the helicopters were themselves receiving intense AAA fire in return. At about 1320 the aircraft piloted by Seagle and Howard completed one pass over the target and was circling to begin another when it was struck by a hail of automatic weapons fire, most probably from yet another ZU-23. The initial impact of the enemy rounds seriously damaged the Sea Cobra's engine and transmission, severed fuel and hydraulic lines, and apparently severed the tail rotor linkage. Nor was the crew unscathed, for Captain Howard's right hand and upper right arm were shattered by the impact of a round, his right femur was also broken, and a piece of shrapnel the size of a golf ball lodged in his throat. The aircraft's radio had also been knocked out, and Captain Howard got no reply when he shouted to Seagle to take control of the Sea Cobra. Howard turned around toward Seagle in the rear cockpit, and saw that his co-pilot was apparently unconscious. The grievously wounded Howard thus had no choice but to attempt to land the stricken aircraft himself.

Howard somehow managed to guide the disintegrating AH-1T to a barely controlled landing on a sports field several hundred meters from the fort, though being safely on the ground was just the beginning of the two pilots' ordeal. The Sea Cobra had landed right side up and, to Captain Howard's surprise and immense relief, it did not explode. However, several small fires within the aircraft's fuselage made it imperative that the two Marines get out with all speed, for the helicopter's remaining fuel and munitions could be expected to detonate at any moment. Captain Seagle had by this time regained consciousness and he pulled Howard out of his seat and away from the now well-alight Sea Cobra. At this point a group of PRA troops opened fire on the two Marines, and Howard implored Seagle to leave and save himself. Seagle did his best to pull his co-pilot to safety behind a nearby stand of trees and then, in an apparent attempt to lead the enemy troops away from Howard, ran toward some buildings near the beach. The seriously wounded Howard then pulled out his emergency radio and began calling for help.

Captain Seagle's attempt to decoy the enemy troops away from Howard was not entirely successful, for though the main body of the pursuing PRA troops ran off after Seagle, one squad continued toward Howard. The enemy troops, whom Howard heard speaking Spanish rather than the English spoken by Grenadians, opened fire on the defenseless Marine, who could only make defiant gestures in reply. Fortunately for Howard the second AH-1T had located the crash site and at that exact moment came swooping down to strafe the advancing enemy. The accurate and devastating fire laid down by Captain Giguere and Lieutenant Sharver drove off the PRA and, apparently, Cuban soldiers, and Howard was able to pull himself deeper into the tree line. Giguere and Sharver orbited the area until called away to provide urgent support for a special operations team pinned down by enemy fire. A few minutes after their departure a CH-46E appeared, landed near Howard and, while door gunners sprayed the surrounding area with suppressive fire, its crew chief scooped up the battered Marine pilot and rushed him aboard the rescue aircraft. Within minutes Howard was under treatment aboard *Guam*, somewhat amazed that he had actually survived. His amazement was later tempered, however, by the news that Captain Seagle had been killed by the PRA and Cuban troops. The Marine pilot's bullet-riddled body was found on the beach near the crash site, a scene that *Newsweek* magazine later callously and graphically portrayed in a photo that accompanied an article about the invasion. And, ironically, the second Sea Cobra was shot down over Grand Anse Bay within an hour of acting as Howard's guardian angel; both John Giguere and J.R. Sharver were killed instantly.

The Ranger forces operating on the southern end of Grenada were also continuing to receive enemy fire, though by 1400 hours the situation around Point Salines was secure enough to allow the landing of the C-141 transports bringing in the lead elements of the 82d Airborne Division. Some 28 MAC C-141 Starlifters and six C-5A Galaxies had departed Pope Air Force Base, North Carolina, earlier that morning carrying men and equipment of the 2d and 3d Battalions of the 82d's 325th Infantry. The huge Galaxies, operated by the 436th Military Airlift Wing from Dover AFB, Delaware, had headed for Grantly Adams Airport in Barbados while the smaller Starlifters, flown by crews from the 437th and 438th MAWs from, respectively, Charleston AFB, South Carolina and McGuire AFB, New Jersey, had made directly for Grenada. The arrival of the C-141s over the island created more than a few problems, not the least of which was how to best organize the landing and takeoff of more than a score of heavily laden aircraft. The runway at Point Salines had no approach or landing lights, was still obstructed for more than a third of its length, and was too narrow to permit more than two aircraft to be on the ground at the same time. Moreover, the entire Point Salines complex was still subject to intermittent automatic weapons and mortar fire, a fact which made anyone familiar with the explosive characteristics of JP-5 aviation fuel more than a little nervous. Still, Army and Air Force air traffic control teams were able to come to grips with these various considerations and the arrival of the 325th Infantry battalions, though occasionally interrupted, continued with reasonable dispatch.

The arrival of the first C-141s undoubtedly helped spur the major PRA assault that developed on the Ranger perimeter north of the airfield just after 1430. The attack began when three BTR-60PBs, supported by infantry with automatic weapons and mortars, attempted to break through the Ranger lines and sweep toward the busy airfield. The PRA assault was slowed by determined Ranger resistance, and two of the three BTRs were knocked out by 90mm recoilless rifle fire. The supporting infantry and remaining BTR turned and attempted to flee, but were subjected to withering Ranger machine gun, rifle and mortar fire. The lone BTR was caught out in the open by either a Navy A-7 Cosair II or an AC-130H, exactly which is not clear, and was destroyed by cannon fire. This marked the end of the abortive PRA counter-attack, and the Point Salines area was once again declared secure. The runway, which had been closed when the attack began, was reopened, and the by now normal arrival and departure schedule was resumed.

The decision to keep Company G, 2/8 Marines aboard the ships of PHIBRON 4, rather than send it ashore in LVTs near Grenville, now proved to be a boon. The special operations forces assigned to capture Fort Frederick, and those that had taken the Governor General's Residence only to be trapped inside by a superior PRA force, were still in deep trouble. It was obvious that they needed help, and Admiral Metcalf therefore decided to dispatch Company G to their aid. Shortly after 1430 the ships of PHIBRON 4, except *Trenton*, which was to stay behind to support the Marine units operating near Grenville, were ordered to move to the west coast of Grenada and conduct yet another landing operation. This time the Marines would indeed go ashore by LVT, via a landing at Grand Mal Bay, and would then move to relieve the special operations forces at Fort

Frederick and the Governor General's Residence.

Shortly after the ships of PHIBRON 4 began their move around the southern end of Grenada, A-7 attack aircraft from *Independence* were called in for yet another air strike near Fort Frederick. The aircraft had been in action over the area for several hours, assisted by AC-130 gunships, yet had not been able to silence several well-sited and bothersome AAA emplacements. The 1530 strike was intended to silence these guns once and for all, and was undertaken by A-7s equipped with bombs, rockets and cannon. One of the pilots, upon completing his run, noted that much of the AA fire seemed to be coming from a large, official looking building near the fort. The structure in question was surrounded by known troop concentrations, and several groups of soldiers had been seen entering and leaving by the main gate. Moreover, a large Grenadian flag was flying from the building which, coupled with the other evidence, seemed conclusive proof that the structure was under PRA control. On a subsequent run an A-7 hit the building, whether intentionally or by accident, with a 500-pound bomb. The structure was later discovered to be a mental hospital; tragically, several civilian patients were killed in the attack.

By the early evening of D-Day the U.S. forces were well entrenched on Grenada, though fierce battles still continued between the Americans and PRA/Cuban troops resisting the landings. The battles around Fort Frederick continued to be of special concern to Admiral Metcalf and his staff, and the relief of those U.S. special operations forces engaged in that area continued to be a high priority. At 1915 the first Marine LVTs began to go ashore near the fuel storage area at Grand Mal Bay, and by 2200 13 vehicles, five M-60 tanks and the men of Company G, 2/8 Marines, were ashore. Over the next few hours the force prepared for the advance on Fort Frederick, where the special operations forces continued their stand against the surrounding PRA units.

26 OCTOBER (D+1)

The second day of Operation URGENT FURY began with two important decisions by the Commander of JTF 120, Vice Admiral Metcalf. First, the unexpectedly stiff resistance put up by the PRA and Cuban forces on Grenada, coupled with American confusion regarding the actual number of enemy combatants on the island, led Metcalf to send a 0200 message to JCS requesting the allocation to his command of four additional battalions of the 82d Airborne Division. The Admiral and his staff believed that the additional troops would allow the American forces to gain control of the island more quickly, and would also provide a force large enough to deal with any military contingency that might develop. Second, Admiral Metcalf decided that the evacuation of American citizens and certain other non-Grenadian nationals should commence at first light, and so informed Washington.

At about the same time Admiral Metcalf's message was being sent to the Pentagon, the men of Company F, 2/8 Marines, began assembling at LZ Oriole near Grenville. The area around the coastal city had been secured on the morning of D-Day, and there was other, more pressing business that required the Marines' attention. At approximately 0245 the men of Company F boarded several Sea Knights of HMM 261, and at 0300 lifted off for LZ Fuel near Grand Mal Bay. There the Marines linked up with Company G and the LVTs and tanks that had landed the preceding night, and the combined force set out for Fort Frederick and the Governor General's Residence. The mere sight of the 60-ton M-60s was apparently enough to scare off those PRA units remaining between the Marines and their objectives, for the Americans did not encounter any resistance. By 0530 Company G had relieved the special operations forces holding the Governor's Residence, while Company F had secured the Queen's Park racecourse and the surrounding area. After consolidating their gains both units then resumed the advance toward Fort Frederick.

The morning of 26 October also began early for the men aboard the *Independence*, for the carrier's air wing was faced with yet another full day of operations. The Navy pilots had been providing close air support for the forces ashore since early on D-Day, and it was expected that the second day of URGENT FURY would be just as busy. The aircraft had to be armed and fueled, while their pilots were briefed on the latest known enemy concentrations. The A-6s and A-7s weren't the only aircraft scheduled to fly that day, however, for the *Independence* was in a war zone and the threat of attack, no matter how remote, still had to be dealt with. Thus the Hawkeyes of VAW-122 and Vikings of VS-28 would be launched on their normal patrols, while the F-14s of VF-14 and VF-32 stood ready to intercept any unidentified aircraft that might attempt to

reach the ships of the task force. Nor were the Sea Kings of HS-15 idle, for they were tasked with such duties as plane guard during the launch of aircraft, as well as with limited Search and Rescue (SAR) activities over and around Grenada itself, in addition to their normal ASW role.

Army and Marine operations ashore continued as planned throughout the morning, though by 1100 it was apparent that a problem was developing on the grounds of the Grand Anse medical school campus. A large number of PRA troops began constructing fortified positions near several of the school buildings, and it was obvious that they intended to resist any American attempt to secure the more than 240 U.S. medical students still present on the campus. The American forces had not learned of the students' presence at the campus until late the preceeding afternoon, and it was therefore becoming increasingly urgent that they be moved from their rather exposed position. The continuing military operations underway all over the island initially made it difficult to assemble the men and machines necessary for a rescue, though by 1545 that afternoon all was in readiness.

A Marine LVTP-7 amphibious armored personnel carrier guards LZ Fuel near Grand Mal Bay on 26 October as a CH-46E prepares to lift off in the background. The LVTP was one of 13 such vehicles that conducted an amphibious landing late the previous evening, carrying ashore the men of Company G, 2/8 Marines. This unit, supported by five M-60 tanks, began advancing on Fort Frederick and the Governor General's Residence a few hours before this photo was taken. DoD

The plan to secure the medical students at Grand Anse was based on a surprise helicopter assault by men of the 2d Ranger Battalion. The Rangers were to be transported to the campus in Marine CH-46s, Army helicopters not yet being present on the island, which would land in cleared areas near the school buildings under covering fire supplied by their own door gunners, A-7s and AC-130s. Once the Rangers had disembarked, the Sea Knights would move to a holding orbit offshore, thereby clearing the landing zone for HMM 261's four CH-53 Sea Stallions. These larger helicopters would then swoop in, take aboard all 240 students, and then transport them to a safe location. The orbiting CH-46s would move back into the LZ as soon as the Sea Stallions left, pick up the Ranger assault force, and make for Point Salines. As it turned out, the operation went almost exactly as planned, though one CH-46 was disabled by enemy fire during the insertion of the Rangers and had to be abandoned on Grand Anse beach. Still, all the students were safely evacuated from the medical school by 1700, and the rescue force sustained only a few injuries. One Ranger squad did have something more of an adventure than had been planned on, however, for the men were inadvertently left behind when the rescue force was withdrawn from the campus area. The squad spent an anxious few hours behind enemy lines, but finally managed to use a life raft from the CH-46 downed on Grand Anse beach to row out to a U.S. vessel offshore.

The rescue of the students at Grand Anse, and the capture of Fort Frederick later that afternoon, were both excellent examples of intra-service operational coordination at its best. In both instances Army, Navy, Marine and Air Force assets worked together to achieve a vital goal. However, American military operations on Grenada on 26 October also provided a grim example of the consequences of non-coordination between combat forces. At approximately 1645 an aircraft from the *Independence* was called on to provide close air support for Army troops that had made contact with enemy forces north of the Point Salines complex. The exact sequence of events remains unclear, but the Navy pilot apparently was either given incorrect target coordinates or was confused as to the location of the enemy troops. For whatever reason, the aircraft accidentally bombed an outpost of the 82d Airborne Division, seriously wounding nine Americans.

Opposite: Company G's advance toward the besieged special operations forces was supported by HMM-261's two surviving AH-1T Sea Cobras, one of which is seen here returning to *Guam* to refuel on the afternoon of 26 October.　　DoD

The only aircraft lost during the Grand Anse rescue operation was this Marine CH-46E. The helicopter was disabled by ground fire during the initial insertion of the Ranger rescue force, and was then abandoned on Grand Anse beach. DoD

This close-up of the downed Marine Sea Knight's cockpit is deceptive, for most of the damage visible here was not caused by enemy fire. After the helicopter was abandoned an AC-130H Spectre gunship strafed it in order to prevent enemy troops from salvaging its weapons, ammunition and other useful equipment. Note, however, that the bolt-on armor plating just aft of the cockpit has done its job by deflecting all but a few incoming rounds. DoD

All 240 students extracted from the Grand Anse campus were flown to Point Salines aboard HMM 261's CH-53D Sea Stallions. Here the four aircraft are seen taxiing toward a reception area where the students were to be off-loaded. DoD

The airlift effort into Grenada continued unabated throughout 26 October. Here an MAC C-130 prepares to taxi out for takeoff just after unloading several tons of equipment at Point Salines. The small dome immediately above and to the rear of the aircraft's cockpit houses the antenna for the C-130's AN/APN-169A intraformation positioning radar. DoD

27 OCTOBER (D+2)

The third day of American operations on Grenada began with an 82d Airborne sweep through the Lance aux Epines peninsula to the east of Point Salines. Despite resistance by PRA and Cuban forces, the U.S. troops were able to locate, secure and evacuate a further 190 American citizens. These individuals were moved to Point Salines where they joined other American and third-country nationals awaiting onward transportation to the U.S. The evacuation effort had begun earlier that morning under the direction of Air Force aerial port detachment personnel and the first group of evacuees had departed for Charleston AFB, South Carolina, just after first light aboard an Air Force Reserve C-141B Starlifter of the 315th MAW. By 0815 more than 350 persons had been dispatched to the continental United States, and scores of others were being processed for departure.

The morning of 27 October also saw the arrival of the lead elements of the four additional 82d Airborne Division battalions requested by Admiral Metcalf. The units, the 1st and 2d battalions of both the 505th and 508th Infantry, would continue to arrive on Grenada throughout the next two days. Some of the incoming troops flew into Point Salines on C-141s directly from Pope AFB, while others were transferred to C-130s at Barbados prior to their arrival on the island. This change in aircraft was necessitated by several factors. First, the runway at Point Salines was still obstructed for part of its length, and C-130s were better able to operate on the short runway than were the larger C-141s. Second, the limited ramp space bordering the runway meant that only three aircraft, two C-130s and a single C-141, could be on the ground at any given time, thus making it advisable to put as many troops as possible aboard C-130s. And, third, the limited number of all-terrain unloading vehicles available at Point Salines meant that it took longer to unload and "turn-around" each C-141 than it did to perform the same tasks for each C-130.

Elements of two important Army aviation units, the 57th Medical Detachment (57th Med Det) and the 82d Airborne Division's 82d Combat Aviation Battalion (82d CAB), also began arriving on Grenada during the morning of 27 October. Both units had been alerted for deployment on 25 October, and both had staged through Pope AFB. At Pope the UH-60 utility helicopters of the 82d CAB's Company B and the specially-equipped Blackhawk aeromedical evacuation (MEDEVAC) aircraft of the 57th Med Det had been partially dismantled and loaded aboard C-5A Galaxies of the 436th MAW, which had then flown the aircraft and their crews and support personnel to Grantly Adams International Airport on Barbados. The Galaxies had arrived at their destination on the evening of the 25th, and the Army personnel spent the rest of that night and all of 26

October reassembling and test flying the UH-60s. By the early morning of 27 October the Blackhawks were judged ready for the 100-mile flight to Grenada, and the 18 82d CAB and three 57th Med Det aircraft were on the ground at Point Salines before dawn. Shortly after their arrival, the Blackhawks of Company B began operational flights in support of U.S. and CPF troops, while the 57th Med Det crews familiarized themselves with MEDEVAC operations of the island. The two groups of UH-60s were soon joined by the 82d CAB's remaining aircraft, the AH-1S Cobras of Company D, the UH-1H C&C helicopters of Company C, and Company A's Blackhawks. Additional aircrews and aircraft, primarily UH-60s, were also apparently supplied by several other Army aviation organizations, though the number of men and aircraft and the units from which they came remain unclear.

Prior to the arrival of the 57th Med Det, aeromedical evacuation activities on Grenada had been conducted by HMM 261 and HS-15, with some assistance probably supplied on 25 October by aviation assets supporting the special operations forces. The Sea Knights, Sea Kings and Sea Stallions of the two naval helicopter squadrons had done yeoman duty in the difficult MEDEVAC role, but they had also been called upon to perform their usual functions and had thus often been torn between several different but equally vital tasks. The arrival of the MEDEVAC-dedicated 57th Med Det Blackhawks was therefore an important step, for it allowed the naval and special operations aircraft to return to their normal duties and replaced them with helicopters especially equipped and crewed for MEDEVAC operations. The Army aircraft took up their new duties almost immediately, and were soon ferrying a stream of U.S., Grenadian, and even Cuban casualties to Army aid stations on shore and to naval vessels lying offshore. But, as important as they were, the Blackhawks were only one part of the overall American aeromedical evacuation effort during URGENT FURY, for their task was essentially the transportation of wounded within the immediate battle area. The onward evacuation of casualties to better-equipped rear area hospitals in Barbados, Puerto Rico and the continental United States was assigned to Navy and Air Force fixed-wing jet aircraft. The Air Force effort was supervised by personnel from the 1st Aeromedical Evacuation Squadron and 375th Aeromedical Airlift Wing, and utilized C-141B Starlifter aircraft configured for litter stowage. The Navy assets involved in aeromedical evacuation were drawn from two Reserve Fleet Logistics Support Squadrons, VR-56 and VR-58, which used specially equipped C-9B Skytrain II aircraft to transport both litter and ambulatory patients to NAS Roosevelt Roads, Puerto Rico and bases on the mainland.

The arrival on Grenada of the 82d CAB was as important to URGENT FURY combat operations as that of the 57th Med Det was to medical

A MAC C-141B taxies down the Point Salines runway under the watchful eyes of 82d Airborne Division paratroopers. The first Starlifters had begun arriving on Grenada on the afternoon of D-Day, and by 27 October the regularity of their arrivals and departures had transformed the Point Salines complex into something resembling a major international airport. Note that the captured Cuban vehicle in the foreground has been prominently marked by its new operators.

Lockheed Aircraft

activities. Prior to the appearance of the 82d CAB Blackhawks the Army had had to rely almost exclusively for operations support on the helicopters of HMM 261 and HS-15, a rather unsatisfactory arrangement which limited the operational flexibility of all concerned. However, the arrival of the Army Blackhawks allowed the Army forces to begin planning for larger-scale and more mobile air assault operations. The first such operation to be conducted following the arrival of the 82d CAB UH-60s was an assault on the large Calivigny Barracks military complex east of Point Salines. The installation was thought to house significant numbers of PRA and Cuban troops, and the task of assaulting and securing it was given to the 2d Ranger Battalion. This unit was to be reinforced with Company A of the 1st Ranger Battalion, and the entire assault force would be inserted by Blackhawks of the 82d CAB's Company B. Prior to the assault the entire Calivigny complex would be "prepped" by naval gunfire, artillery and air strikes, and Navy attack aircraft and AC-130s would be on call to provide any close air support that might be required. Other than enemy opposition the major obstacle that confronted the Blackhawk pilots was the confined nature of the only available landing zones. Each of the few suitable open areas was subject to fire from the six ZU-23 mounts sited in and near the tree lines, and the relatively restricted area of the compound itself dictated that all of the assaulting UH-60s land within a rather constricted zone. To deal with these problems the Ranger and 82d Airborne planners decreed that the Blackhawks would approach the LZ from the southern, seaward side in flights of four, with each wave of aircraft trailing the preceding one by as short a time as possible. The Blackhawks in each flight were to approach, land, unload and lift-off almost as a single element, thereby putting the maximum number of troops into the LZ in the least amount of time.

The air assault on the Calivigny complex got underway at approximately 1600 following the cessation of the naval gunfire, artillery and air strike preparation. The first flight of four aircraft, which carried the individual radio call signs CHALK 1 through CHALK 4, came into the LZ in a diamond formation with CHALK 1 leading, CHALK 2 and 3 slightly behind and to either side, and CHALK 4 to the rear. Enemy fire was relatively light until the four helicopters began to flare for landing, at which point the Blackhawks were engaged by automatic weapons firing from about 40 meters to their front. Both CHALK 1 and CHALK 2 landed without difficulty but the pilot of CHALK 3, Warrant Officer Thomas Speakes, was hit by enemy fire and his aircraft slewed out of position and collided with CHALK 2. The collision effectively destroyed both aircraft outright, killed two men, and seriously wounded seven others. CHALK 4 only managed to avoid the wreckage of the two preceeding aircraft by diving away sharply to the right and crashlanding 35 feet further into the

Grantly Adams International Airport on Barbados was the southern terminus of all C-5A Galaxy operations during URGENT FURY. Here a Galaxy of the 436th MAW disgorges an Army AH-1S Cobra helicopter it has ferried from the continental U.S. Note the empty 2.75-inch rocket launcher and TOW missile cells on the Cobra's stub wings.
Lockheed Aircraft

LZ. CHALK 1 was able to offload its troops and lift off without damage, and the following flight of Blackhawks avoided the crash site by landing their troops at the extreme southern end of the debris-littered LZ. The Rangers went on to secure the Calivigny complex by 1800, having encountered only a few scattered PRA and Cuban troops. The Americans held the area until early the following day, and were then extracted by Company B's remaining UH-60s. A Marine CH-53D then sling-loaded the remains of CHALK 2 and 3 and carried them back to Point Salines.

C-130 traffic into Point Salines rivaled in volume that of the C-141s. Here a MAC Hercules makes its final approach watched by a group of Cuban prisoners and their American guards. Within a few days these same Cubans would themselves be aboard C-130s and C-141s, bound for Barbados and ultimate repatriation to Cuba.

DoD

Top Left: After being reassembled and test flown on Barbados, Army helicopters ferried from the U.S. were flown on to Grenada. Here an AH-1S of the 1/17 Cavalry makes a low pass over a UH-60A Blackhawk dispersal area near Point Salines.   DoD

Top Right: UH-60A Blackhawks of the 82d CAB began operational flights almost immediately after their arrival on Grenada. Here three aircraft of the battalion's Company B embark Jamaican troops of the Caribbean Peacekeeping Forces at Point Salines. Note that each aircraft is equipped with 7.62mm M-60 machine guns mounted in the open windows just aft of the cockpit. The UH-60 is capable of embarking up to 14 fully equipped troops in addition to its three- to four-man crew.   DoD

Bottom: 82d CAB Blackhawks also served as interim MEDEVAC aircraft prior to the arrival of the 57th Med Det. Here an 82d CAB UH-60 arrives aboard *Guam* with patients requiring treatment in the ship's small intensive care unit.   DoD

Top Left: Marine and Navy helicopters also aided in MEDEVAC duties on Grenada during the course of URGENT FURY. Here crewmen from an HMM-261 CH-53D carry a casualty from their aircraft to a forward aid station. DoD

Top Right: A 57th Med Det MEDEVAC Blackhawk awaits its next call on the afternoon of 27 October. Three of the unit's specially equipped aircraft had arrived on Grenada earlier that morning, and all were flying operational sorties that same day. DoD

Bottom: The onward evacuation of casualties to Barbados, Puerto Rico and the continental U.S. was undertaken by Air Force and Navy fixed-wing aircraft. Here a Navy C-9B Skytrain II of Fleet Logistics Support Squadron 58 (VR-58) prepares for departure from Point Salines. DoD

Left: The evacuation of U.S. nationals from Grenada began on the morning of 27 October. By 0815 on that day more than 315 persons, the vast majority of them medical students like the individuals shown here boarding a MAC C-141B, had departed for the United States.   DoD

Bottom: A more complete view of a C-9B. The Skytrain II is a military transport version of the McDonnell-Douglas DC-9 Series 30 commercial airliner, and has been in service with the Navy since 1973.

McDonnell-Douglas Aircraft

A C-141B of the 63d MAW, Norton AFB, California, departs Point Salines with a load of evacuees on the afternoon of 27 October.   DoD

This photo graphically illustrates that Army helicopter operations on Grenada were not conducted without loss. Three of the UH-60s in this photograph were disabled during the same action: the air assault on the Calivigny Barracks complex on the afternoon of 27 October.   DoD

28 OCTOBER (D+3)

By the morning of 28 October it was obvious that the combat phase of Operation URGENT FURY was nearing an end. Though some PRA, PRM and Cuban troops remained at large, the vast majority had already been captured, killed, or forced to abandon their weapons and uniforms and attempt to find shelter among an unsympathetic and non-supportive civilian population. This virtual collapse of enemy resistance on Grenada did not result in a cessation of U.S. and CPF military activities, however, for large segments of the island still had to be thoroughly searched for weapons caches and fugitive enemy troops. Elements of the 82d Airborne therefore continued their sweep of the Lance aux Epines peninsula, while Marine units patrolled the central and northern sections of the island. Army, Navy and Marine Corps aircraft played a major role in these search and clear operations by transporting troops, performing aerial reconnaissance, evacuating wounded friendly and enemy troops and ill or injured civilians, and carrying the equipment and supplies needed by the units in the field. In one of the more unusual instances of cooperative effort between aircraft and ground troops, a UH-1H Iroquois C&C helicopter of the 82d CAB's Company C helped capture the fugitive General Hudson Austin by hovering directly above the house in which Austin and a few supporters were attempting to hide. The on-scene infantry commander later credited the helicopter's presence with dispiriting the PRA leader to the point of surrender.

Air Force aircraft continued to play a variety of important roles in URGENT FURY as well, with one of the more interesting being that of supporting psychological warfare operations (PSYOPs) aimed at influencing the attitudes and emotions of Grenada's civilian population.

The effective collapse of enemy resistance on Grenada did not result in a lessening of American aviation operations on the island, for U.S. forces continued to conduct search and clear sweeps and helicopters continued to be the most effective mode of transportation. Here a flight of Army Blackhawks departs Point Salines on 28 October at the start of another such sweep. DoD

Both Army and Navy PSYOPs teams had been actively at work on Grenada since D-Day, and they had routinely called upon Air Force aircraft to drop millions of printed information leaflets across the entire island. These leaflet drops were conducted primarily by MC-130E aircraft of the 1st SOW, and continued well into 28 October. Another type of PSYOPs mission, that of the airborne broadcast by loudspeaker of prerecorded information and the re-transmission of low-power radio programming, was conducted by specially-equipped EC-130E "Coronet Solo II" electronic warfare and surveillance aircraft of the Pennsylvania Air National Guard's 193d Electronic Combat Group.

Not all aviation activities on Grenada during this fourth day of URGENT FURY were as exotic, however. Indeed, for most American aircraft and aircrew on and near the island 28 October was simply more of "business as usual." For the MAC C-141s and C-130s business was mostly shuttling people, both military and civilian. The evacuation of American citizens and other third-country nationals continued apace, and by 0900 over 450 evacuees had been dispatched to the continental United States.

29 OCTOBER AND AFTER

AMERICAN AND CPF TROOPS CONTINUED THEIR SWEEP AND CLEAR operations on 29 October, and just before noon a patrol from H Battery, 3/10 Marines, captured Bernard Coard and several other important fugitives. Early the next morning a motorized patrol from Company E, 2/8 Marines, entered and secured Sauteurs, and just before 1300 82d Airborne units occupied the Fort Jeudy area without resistance. Later that same day Marines of Company G secured Goyuave, also without encountering enemy opposition, after which they occupied the Victoria area. In each of these cases the ground forces were supported by both helicopters and fixed-wing aircraft. The 82d CAB's Blackhawks, often escorted by AH-1S gunships, provided troop lift and logistical resupply support for Army and CPF units, while other UH-60, AH-1S, OH-58C and UH-1H aircraft undertook a range of reconnaissance, observation, and C&C tasks. The AH-1T, CH-46E, CH-53D and UH-1N helicopters of HMM 261 provided similar support for Marine forces engaged in sweep and clear operations in central and northern Grenada. In addition, Army, Navy and Marine helicopters all played a role in off-shore search and rescue (SAR) and patrol activities, as did Air Force AC-130H and Navy S-3A and E-2C aircraft. The 57th Med Det's specially equipped Blackhawks continued to ferry the ill and injured to aid stations on shore and to ships just off the coast, while Air Force C-130 and C-141 and Navy C-9B transports kept up their daily shuttle flights to Barbados, Puerto

Nor was the flow of people just one way, for the Air Force transports continued to carry men and equipment into Grenada throughout the day. By far the largest mass arrival concerned elements of the 2d Battalion, 505th Infantry, which were flown into Point Salines by C-141 and C-130 beginning just after 1100. Elements of yet another Army aviation unit, the 1st Squadron, 17th Cavalry (1/17 CAV) also began arriving on Grenada during this period. This Fort Bragg-based organization deployed its Headquarters and Headquarters Troop (HHT), A Troop and B Troop with a mix of UH-1H, OH-58C and AH-1S aircraft. Later in the evening the ramp at Point Salines filled with aircraft bringing in the sixth and last 82d Airborne infantry battalion committed to URGENT FURY, the 2d of the 508th. The arrival of this unit was somewhat delayed, however, by the departure of aircraft bearing the 1st and 2d Ranger Battalions. The very special skills practiced by these elite units were no longer required on Grenada and they had therefore been released for redeployment to the continental U.S.

Rico and the continental U.S. Nor were the Air Force's PSYOPS-dedicated EC- and MC-130E aircraft idle, for they continued their leaflet and radio broadcast flights throughout 29 and 30 October.

On the morning of 30 October Marine units had also begun turning their positions over to Army and CPF troops as a prelude to redeployment aboard the ships of PHIBRON 4. This "backloading" of the Marines was itself a preliminary to yet another assault, for the 22d MAU had been tasked with securing the island of Carriacou. The island, a Grenadian possession 40 miles north of Grenada itself, was thought to be garrisoned by a significant number of well-armed PRA troops. The plan for the Marine assault thus hinged on surprise landings by both amphibious vehicles and helicopters. The Marines were to be transported to the island aboard *Guam* and her accompanying landing ships, and the assault was to make use of HMM 261's helicopters and the A-6E and A-7E strike aircraft aboard *Independence*. The carrier's movement away from Grenada, and her projected departure for Lebanon once the assault was successfully concluded, was of some concern to senior U.S. commanders for it would remove attack aircraft that might conceivably be needed should hostilities resume. In order to allay these apprehensions 12 Air Force A-10A Thunderbolt II attack aircraft of the 23d TFW were moved from England AFB, Louisiana, to Barbados on 30 October. There they were tasked with providing any close air support that might be required on Grenada.

All Marine forces had completed backloading aboard the ships of

An Air Force C-130 unloads Army equipment in front of the Pearls airport terminal building prior to the withdrawal of the Marine units that had originally secured the complex. The airport was unofficially renamed Marine Corps Air Station Douglas (after a popular Sergeant Major killed a few days earlier in the Beirut bombing), hence the sign.

DoD

PHIBRON 4 by 2000 on 31 October, and the assault on the small island began at 0430 the following morning. The Marines did not encounter any resistance, and Carriacou was reported secure by 1055. The landing forces spent the remainder of the day searching for arms caches and fugitive PRA members, and began backloading aboard ship the following morning. The departing Marines were replaced on Cariacou by CPF and Army troops, and just after 1600 on 2 November MARG 1-84 and the *Independence* carrier battle group departed the area for the Mediterranean.

The second day of November also brought about other significant events in the history of Operation URGENT FURY, for at 1500 Admiral Metcalf determined that hostilities on Grenada had officially ended. This announcement did not lessen the pace of American aviation activities on and near the island, however, for much remained to be done. One of the more interesting tasks begun that day was the on-going evacuation of Cuban POWs and wounded. The first Cubans and five representatives of the International Red Cross boarded MAC C-130s at Point Salines and were flown to Grantly Adams Airport on Barbados. There the Cubans and their escorts were put aboard aircraft of Cubana airlines for the onward flight to Havana. The former commander of all Cuban forces on Grenada was among the last to be repatriated. Though initially received as a hero he was later courtmartialed for cowardice under fire and for allowing the American and CPF forces to defeat the PRA/Cuban coalition. He was stripped of his rank and sent to serve with the Cuban expeditionary forces in Angola.

Twelve Air Force A-10A Thunderbolt II attack aircraft were deployed to Barbados following the departure of the *Independence* and her embarked air wing. The A-10s, identical to the one illustrated here, were drawn from the 23d TFW at England AFB, Louisiana, and tasked with providing close air support over Grenada in the unlikely event of renewed hostilities. The cylindrical object protruding from the lower part of the aircraft's nose is the muzzle of the A-10's immense GAU-8/A 7-barrelled 30mm cannon, and the squared pod extending downward from the fuselage directly below the cockpit houses the Pave Penny laser target designator.   USAF

EPILOG

THE OFFICIAL CESSATION OF HOSTILITIES ON 2 NOVEMBER MARKED THE beginning of a gradual decline in American air operations on and near Grenada as aircraft were redeployed to their home bases. The last 1st SOW aircraft dedicated to URGENT FURY operations returned to the United States on 2 November, as did the Pennsylvania Air National Guard's EC-130E "Coronet Solo II" aircraft. The C-130s and C-141s that had provided the bulk of URGENT FURY military airlift support also began turning to other tasks, as did the Dover, Delaware-based C-5A Galaxies of the 436th and 512th MAWs. The 23d TFW A-10s that had been deployed to Barbados to provide on-call close air support after the departure of the *Independence* carrier battle group had not been required to fire their guns in anger, and they too departed for home soon after the official cessation of hostilities.

The Army aircraft deployed to Grenada to support URGENT FURY also began returning to the United States shortly after 2 November. The 82d CAB began its redeployment within two weeks of that date, and the entire unit had returned to Fort Bragg by 22 November. The MEDEVAC Blackhawks of the 57th Med Det continued to fly mercy missions on Grenada well into December, then they too began departing for home. Some Army helicopters remained on the island to support ongoing U.S. military and political missions, however, and it is likely that there will be at least a token Army aviation presence for some time to come.

For the Navy and Marine Corps aircraft that participated in the assault on Grenada the end of URGENT FURY did not mean the end of combat operations. After departing the Caribbean the ships of PHIBRON 4 and the *Independence* carrier battle group moved into the Mediterranean and took up positions off the coast of Lebanon. Once there the aircraft of Carrier Air Wing 6 began flying operational missions in support of U.S. and other Multinational Peacekeeping Force units in and around Beirut. In early December A-6E and A-7E strike aircraft from VA-15, VA-87 and VA-176 were directed to attack Syrian anti-aircraft sites in central Lebanon. In the ensuing strike two Navy aircraft, one A-7 and one A-6, were shot down, resulting in the death of one pilot and the capture of another.

Operation URGENT FURY marked the first large-scale, multi-service combat use of American airpower since the end of the Vietnam War and, as such, it provides a unique opportunity to assess the strengths and weaknesses of current U.S. military aircraft and aviation doctrine. Though a thorough examination of these topics is beyond the scope of this work, mention should be made of three important lessons learned from aviation activities in Grenada.

First, American aircraft engaged in URGENT FURY operations performed, for the most part, very well. The UH-60 Blackhawk, for example, showed itself to be a worthy successor to the famous UH-1 "Huey" family of utility helicopters. The value of the AC-130H in the suppression of enemy anti-aircraft sites and the provision of accurate on-call close air support was re-discovered, as was the importance of having MEDEVAC-dedicated aircraft available in the battle area from the first day of contact. And, perhaps most importantly, the essential work well performed by Air Force C-130s, C-141s and C-5s demonstrates yet again the need for a global power like the United States to develop and maintain its military airlift capacity.

Second, the successful employment of more than 107 military helicopters during URGENT FURY, and the loss in combat of just nine of those aircraft,* demonstrates that rotary wing aircraft do indeed have a place in the military inventory. However, it must also be remembered that the anti-aircraft threat encountered by U.S. helicopters over Grenada, though deadly at times, was essentially primitive. The ZU-23 cannon and multi-barrel heavy machine guns which formed the core of the AAA threat were not radar-directed, nor did the Grenadian military have access to the more sophisticated weapons systems that are currently in use by those powers the U.S. considers to be its most likely adversaries in any large-scale war. It is therefore imprudent, if not overtly dangerous, to make sweeping generalizations about the modern military helicopter's ability to survive over the space-age battlefield, for the AAA threat on Grenada in no way resembled the highly sophisticated interlocking array of gun and missile systems that would be encountered during the course of a full-scale conventional war. The same is equally true for fixed-wing gunships and assault transport aircraft; they are valuable assets under certain conditions, but their usefulness would rapidly diminish if they were

---

*These are the figures officially released by the Department of Defense. The nine aircraft counted as lost by DoD included 2 AH-1T Sea Cobras, 1 CH-46E Sea Knight and 1 UH-60A Blackhawk completely destroyed and five UH-60A Blackhawks so severely damaged that they required depot or intermediate maintenance level repairs.

forced to operate over a battlefield dominated by a modern air defense network.

The third and final lesson to be learned from the air operations conducted during URGENT FURY concerns the value of the modern "big-deck" aircraft carrier. During the course of the Grenada operation the USS *Independence* ably demonstrated that a modern carrier battle group is still the most effective platform for the projection of U.S. military power and the protection of U.S. interests abroad. The carrier was able to provide on-call close air support to forces ashore while at the same time maintaining her anti-submarine, electronic surveillance and airborne early warning functions, all on an around-the-clock basis. She was able to accomplish these tasks because she carried the right mix of aircraft, and was capable of undertaking sustained operations far removed from the continental United States. An important point to remember, however, is that the *Independence* carried out these varied tasks during the course of a tactically limited military operation. Her usefulness might well have been severely degraded had she been forced to perform while under the sort of continuous air, surface and subsurface attack that would characterize a clash between American and Soviet naval forces.

The preceding cautionary reflections on the limitations of various weapons systems are not intended to detract in any way from the accomplishments of American airmen in Grenada. The air operations undertaken during the course of URGENT FURY were, for the most part, well-planned and well-executed examples of modern combat flying. The Army, Navy, Marine Corps and Coast Guard pilots and aircrew that participated in the assault overcame often-poor weather, enemy fire, inadequate facilities, mechanical malfunctions and occasional poor planning to achieve some spectacular successes. Without their skill, courage and dedication, Operation URGENT FURY might well have had a different and far less acceptable outcome.

American troops began withdrawing from Grenada soon after the end of hostilities, and the vast majority departed by air. Here troops of the 82d Airborne Division board a MAC C-141B Starlifter for the return flight to Fort Bragg, via Pope AFB, North Carolina.   Lockheed Aircraft

APPENDIX A:
American Military Aviation Units That Took Part in URGENT FURY *

SECTION 1: AIR FORCE

Military Airlift Command

Unit	Home Station	Aircraft Type
314th TAW	Little Rock AFB, AR	C-130E
317th TAW	Pope AFB, NC	C-130E
459th TAW	Andrews AFB, MD	C-130E
463d TAW	Dyess AFB, TX	C-130H
60th MAW	Travis AFB, CA	C-141B
62d MAW	McChord AFB, WA	C-141B
63d MAW	Norton AFB, CA	C-141B
315th MAW	Charleston AFB, SC	C-141B
436th MAW	Dover AFB, DE	C-5A
437th MAW	Charleston AFB, SC	C-141B
438th MAW	McGuire AFB, NJ	C-141B
512th MAW	Dover AFB, DE	C-5A
514th MAW	McGuire AFB, NJ	C-141B
913th TAG	NAS Willow Grove, PA	C-130E
1st SOW	Hurlbert Field, FL	AC-130H MC-130E
193d ECG	Harrisburg IAP, PA	EC-130E

Tactical Air Command

Unit	Home Station	Aircraft Type
23d TFW	England AFB, LA	A-10A
33d TFW	Eglin AFB, FL	F-15A
552d AWCD	Tinker AFB, OK	E-3A

Strategic Air Command

Unit	Home Station	Aircraft Type
2d BW	Barksdale AFB, LA	KC-10A

SECTION 2: ARMY

Unit	Home Station	Aircraft Type
160th Aviation Bn	Fort Campbell, KY	OH-6 Cayuse 500MD Defender

---

*These organizations are known to have supplied personnel, aircraft, or both, to the U.S. effort. Not all assets of each unit were necessarily employed during URGENT FURY.

82d Combat Avn Bn	Fort Bragg, NC	
Companies A & D		UH-60A Blackhawk
Company C		UH-1H Iroquois
Company D		AH-1S Cobra
1st Sqdn, 17th Cav	Fort Bragg, NC	
H&H Troop		UH-1H Iroquois
A Troop		OH-58C Kiowa
B Troop		AH-1S Cobra
57th Medical Det	Fort Bragg, NC	UH-60A Blackhawk
101st Avn Group	Fort Campbell, KY	UH-60A Blackhawk

SECTION 3: NAVY

Carrier Air Wing 6 (embarked aboard USS *Independence*)

VA-15	NAS Cecil Field, FL	12 A-7E Corsair II
VA-87	NAS Cecil Field, FL	12 A-7E Corsair II
VA-176	NAS Oceana, VA	10 A-6E Intruder
		4 KA-6D tanker
VF-14	NAS Oceana, VA	12 F-14A Tomcat
VF-32	NAS Oceana, VA	12 F-14A Tomcat
VS-28	NAS Cecil Field, FL	10 S-3A Viking
VAQ-131	NAS Oceana, VA	4 EA-6B Prowler
VAW-122	NAS Norfolk, VA	4 E-2C Hawkeye
HS-15	NAS Jacksonville, FL	6 SH-3H Sea King

Non-carrier assets

| VR-56 | NAS Jacksonville, FL | 2 C-9B Skytrain II |
| VR-58 | NAS Norfolk, VA | 2 C-9B Skytrain II |

SECTION 4: MARINE CORPS (embarked aboard USS *Guam*)

HMM-261	MCAS New River, NC	12 CH-46E Sea Knight
		4 CH-53D Sea Stallion
		4 AH-1T Sea Cobra
		2 UH-1N Huey

SECTION 5: COAST GUARD

At least two Coast Guard C-130H aircraft (numbers 1700 and 1701) are known to have participated in URGENT FURY-related SAR and equipment transport missions. Both aircraft are based at CGAS Miami, FL. It is also likely that other Coast Guard aircraft, most probably HU-25 Guardian maritime surveillance aircraft or HH-3F Pelican SAR helicopters, undertook Grenada-related tasks.

APPENDIX B:
Specifications of Aircraft That Participated in Operation URGENT FURY

SECTION 1: NON-AMERICAN AIRCRAFT

Key:
WGS = Wing Span
WGA = Wing Area (sq. ft.)
LNG = Length Overall

MLS = Maximum Level Speed
SCL = Service Ceiling
NRG = Normal Range

CN = Cannon
MG = Machine Gun
RK = Unguided Rocket

Aircraft	Type	Builder	Accommodation	Powerplant	Dimensions	Performance	Armament
AN-2P Colt	Light Utility Transport	Antonov Aircraft Kiev, USSR	2-3 Crew 10-14 passenger	1 Shvetsov ASh-62-1R Radial	WGS: 59'8" (top) WGA: 765' LNG: 42'6"	MLS: 158 mph SCL: 14,300' NRG: 500 mi	none normally fitted
AN-26B Curl	Medium Transport	as above	5 Crew, 40 troops/pass	2 Ivchenko AI-24VT Turboprops	WGS: 95'9" WGA: 807' LNG: 78'1"	MLS: 285 mph SCL: 25,000' NRG: 850 mi	none normally fitted

SECTION 2: ROTARY WING AIRCRAFT

Key:
SCL = Service Ceiling

MRD = Main Rotor Diameter
MG = Machine Gun

MLS = Maximum Level Speed
LNG = Length Overall

CN = Cannon
NRG = Normal Range

TRD = Tail Rotor Diameter
RK = Unguided Rocket

Aircraft	Type	Builder	Accommodation	Powerplant	Dimensions	Performance	Armament
AH-1S Cobra	Attack	Bell Helicopter-Textron, Inc. Ft. Worth, TX	2 Crew	1 X T53-L-703 Turboshaft	MRD: 44'0" TRD: 8'6" LNG: 52'11½"	MLS: 140 mph SCL: 12,200 ft. NRG: 305 mi	1 X 20mm cn, 4 X TOW ATM, mg pods, RKs
AH-1T Sea Cobra	Attack	as above	as above	2 X GE T700-GE-700 Turboshaft	MRD: 48'0" TRD: 9'8½" LNG: 58'0"	MLS: 172 mph SCL: 7,400' NRG: 261 mi	as above
CH-46E Sea Knight	Medium Utility Transport	Boeing-Vertol Co. Philadelphia, PA	3 Crew 25 Troops	2 X GE T58-GE-16 Turboshaft	MRD: 51'0" TRD: — LNG: 84'4"	MLS: 170 mph SCL: 14,000' NRG: 250 mi.	2 X .50 MG
CH-53D Sea Stallion	Heavy Utility Transport	Sikorsky Aircraft Stratford, CT	3-4 Crew 40-50 Troops	2 X GE T64-GE-413 Turboshaft	MRD: 72'3" TRD: 16'0" LNG: 88'0"	MLS: 196 mph SCL: 21,000' NRG: 300 mi	2-3 .50 MG
500MD Defender	Observation	Hughes Helicopter Culver City, CA	2-3 Crew	1 X Allison T63-A-720 Trbsft	MRD: 26'5" TRD: 4'3" LNG: 30'6"	MLS: 175 mph SCL: 15,000' NRG: 300 mi	1-2 MG pod, 1 X 40mm Gren lnchr, RKs
OH-58C Kiowa	C&C/ Observation	Bell Helicopter-Textron, Inc. Ft. Worth, TX	2-3 Crew	1 Allison T63-A-720 Turboshaft	MRD: 35'4" TRD: 5'2" LNG: 40'11"	MLS: 138 mph SCL: 18,900' NRG: 290 mi.	2 X MG pod, 1 X 7.62mm MG, RKs
SH-3H Sea King	ASW/ Utility	Sikorsky Aircraft Stratford, CT	4-7 Crew	2 GE T58-GE-10 Turboshaft	MRD: 62'0" TRD: 10'7" LNG: 72'8"	MLS 166 mph SCL: 14,700' NRG: 620 mi.	ASW Torpedoes, 1-2 .50 MG
UH-1H Iroquois	C&C/ Utility	Bell Helicopter-Textron, Inc. Ft. Worth, TX	3 Crew 11 Troops	1 Avco Lycoming T53-L-13 Turboshaft	MRD: 48'0" TRD: 8'6" LNG: 57'9"	MLS: 140 mph SCL: 13,500' NRG: 400 mi.	2 X 7.62 MG
UH-1N	C&C/ Utility	as above	as above	2 PW of Canada PT6 Turboshaft in "Twin Pac"	MRD: 48'2" TRD: 8'6" LNG: 57'3"	MLS: 115 mph SCL: 14,200' NRG: 260 mi	2 X 7.62mm MG or 2 X .50 MG
UH-60A Blackhawk	Medium Utility	Sikorsky Aircraft Stratford, CT	3 Crew 11-14 Troops	2 GE T700-GE-700 Turboshafts	MRD: 53'8" TRD: 11'0" LNG: 64'10"	MLS: 184 mph SCL: 19,000' NRG: 370 mi	2 X 7.62mm MG or 2 X .50 MG

SECTION 3: FIXED-WING AIRCRAFT

Key:
WGS = Wing Span MLS = Maximum Level Speed CN = Cannon
WGA = Wing Area (sq. ft.) SCL = Service Ceiling MG = Machine Gun
LNG = Length Overall NRG = Normal Range RK = Unguided Rocket

Aircraft	Type	Builder	Accommodation	Powerplant	Dimensions	Performance	Armament
A-6E Intruder	Attack	Grumman Aerospace Bethpage, NY	2 Crew	2 Pratt & Whitney J52-P-408 Turbojet	WGS: 53'0" WGA: 528' LNG: 59'10"	MLS: 644 mph SCL: 42,400' NRG: 2000 mi	Up to 18,000 lb. of bombs, RKs, CN-MG pods, etc
A-7E Corsair II	Attack	Vought Division of LTV, Inc. Dallas, TX	1 Crew	1 Allison (RR) TF-41-A2 Turbofan	WGS: 38'9" WGA: 375' LNG: 46'1"	MLS: 690 mph SCL: 40,000' NRG: 800 mi	1 X 20mm CN, Up to 15,000 lb of ordnance
A-10A Thunderbolt II	Attack	Fairchild-Republic Div. of Fairchild, Farmingdale, NY	1 Crew	2 GE TF-34-GE-100 Turbofan	WGS: 57'6" WGA: 506' LNG: 53'4"	MLS: 430 mph SCL: — NRG: 700 mi	1 X 30mm CN, Up to 16,000 lb of ordnance
C-5A Galaxy	Heavy Transport	Lockheed-Georgia Div. of Lockheed Marietta, GA	5 Crew up to 340 trps	4 GE TF39-GE-1C Turbofan	WGS: 222'8" WGA: 6200' LNG: 247'10"	MLS: 570 mph SCL: 35,750' NRG: 2,730 mi	none
C-9B Skytrain II	Utility Transport	Douglas Division of McDonnell-Doug. Long Beach, CA	5 Crew, up to 90 Troops	2 Pratt & Whitney JT8D-9 Turbofans	WGS: 93'5" WGA: 1000' LNG: 119'3"	MLS: 575 mph SCL: 35,000' NRG: 2,800 mi	none
EC/MC/C-130E Hercules	EW, Assault Transport	Lockheed-Georgia Div. of Lockheed Marietta, GA	5 Crew, up to 90 Troops (not in EW version)	4 Allison T56-A-7A Turboprop	WGS: 132'7" WGA: — LNG: 97'9"	MLS: 346 mph SCL: 33,000' NRG: 2,350 mi	none normally fitted
AC-130H Spectre	Attack	as above	14-17 Crew	4 Allison T56-A-15 Turboprop	WGS: 132'7" WGA: — LNG: 97'9"	MLS: 386 mph SCL: 35,000' NRG: 2,450 mi	2 X 7.62mm MG, 2 X 20mm CN, 1 X 40mm CN, 1 105mm
C-141B Starlifter	Medium Transport	as above	5-9 Crew, up to to 210 Troops	4 Pratt & Whitney TF33-P-7 Turbofan	WGS: 159'11" WGA: — LNG: 168'3"	MLS: 566 mph SCL: 40,000' NRG: 2,900 mi	none
E-2C Hawkeye	AEW	Grumman Aerospace Bethpage, NY	5 Crew	2 Allison T56-A-425 Turboprops	WGS: 80'7" WGA: 700' LNG: 57'6"	MLS: 372 mph SCL: 30,800' NRG: 1,600 mi	none normally fitted
E-3A Sentry	AEW	Boeing Aerospace Kent, WA	17+ Crew	4 Pratt & Whitney TF33-PW-100/100A Turbofan	WGS: 145'9" WGA: — LNG: 152'11"	MLS: 530 mph SCL: 29,000' NRG: —	none normally fitted
EA-6B Prowler	EW	Grumman Aerospace Bethpage, NY	4 Crew	2 Pratt & Whitney J52-P-408 Turbojet	WGS: 53'0" WGA: 528' LNG: 59'10"	MLS: 610 mph SCL: 38,000' NRG: 1,100 mi	none normally fitted
F-14A Tomcat	Fighter	as above	2 Crew	2 Pratt & Whitney TF-30-P-412A Turbofan	WGS: 64'1" WGA: 565' LNG: 62'8"	MLS: 1,540 mph SCL: 56,000' NRG: 2,000 mi	1 X 20mm CN, 4 X AIM-7F AAMs; 14,000
F-15C Eagle	Fighter	McDon. Arcrft Div, McDonnell-Doug. St. Louis, MO	1 Crew	2 Pratt & Whitney F100-PW-100 Turbofan	WGS: 42'9" WGA: 608' LNG: 63'9"	MLS: 2.5 Mach SCL: 65,000' NRG: 2,800 mi	1 X 20mm CN, 4 X AIM-9L A 4 X AIM-7F
KC-10A Extender	Tanker/ Transport	Douglas Div of McDonnell-Douglas Long Beach, CA	3 Crew, plus troops/cargo	3 GE CF6-50C2 Turbofan	WGS: 165;4" WGA: 3958' LNG: 181'9"	MLS: 528 mph SCL: 42,000' NRG: 4,000 mi	none
S-3A Viking	ASW	Lockheed-California Div of Lockheed, Burbank, CA	4 Crew	2 GE T34-GE-2 Turbofan	WGS: 68'8" WGA: 598' LNG: 53'4"	MLS: 506 mph SCL: 35,000' NRG: 2,300 mi	various type of torpedoes bombs, RKs